AGRICULTURAL SURPLUS AND RESOURCE MOBILISATION

AGRICULTURAL SURPLUS AND RESOURCE MOBILISATION

VIPLA CHOPRA

ANMOL PUBLICATIONS PVT. LTD.
NEW DELHI-110 002 (INDIA)

ANMOL PUBLICATIONS PVT. LTD.
4374/4B, Ansari Road, Darya Ganj,
New Delhi-110 002

Agricultural Surplus and Resource Mobilisation

First Edition 1997

ISBN 81-7488-457-2

PRINTED IN INDIA

Published by J. L. Kumar for Anmol Publications Pvt. Ltd., New Delhi-110 002 and Printed at Mehra Offset Press, Delhi.

Contents

Preface ix

Acknowledgements xi

PART A

1. Role of Agriculture in Economic Development 2
2. Concept of 'Surplus' and its Measurement Problems 19

PART B

3. Terms of Trade 34
4. Marketed Surplus and Marketable Surplus 50
5. Taxation and Expenditure Benefits 64

PART C

6. Agricultural Surplus and its Mobilization: A Case Study of Punjab 84

Appendices 142

Bibliography 177

Preface

Mobilization of agricultural surpluses is the sine qua non of economic development of a country. In most countries, the channelling of agricultural surpluses has been responsible for the take-off of the economies. Such has been the case, for example, in Japan in 1868, Russia in 1917 and China in 1948. These countries effectively mobilized surpluses through different methods. Thus in the scheme of inter-sectoral flow of surpluses in a developing economy, a crucial role is assigned to the mobilization of agricultural surpluses. In the words of Simon Kuznets, "One of the crucial problems of modern economic growth is how to extract from the product of agriculture a surplus for the financing of capital formation necessary for the industrial growth without at the same time blighting the growth of agriculture, under conditions where no easy quid pro quo for the surplus is available in the country".

In India, agricultural sector occupies a dominant place in the economy. Therefore, the problem of existence and mobilization of agricultural surplus becomes rather significant. The basic issues in connection with the problem are (i) defining the concept of 'surplus', (ii) its measurement and (iii) different methods of its mobilization. There have been a few isolated studies in India examining one of the other issue regarding mobilization of agricultural surplus but no comprehensive study has been dealing with all the components of the problem together.

An attempt has been made in the present study to analyse and examine, both theoretically and empirically, all the major issues of surplus mobilization. This study is based on my Ph. D. dissertation entitled "Mobilization of Agricultural Surpluses in Punjab from 1967-68 to 1981-82". The study has been divided into three parts. In Part A, the first chapter deals with the role of agriculture in economic development. The second chapter presents various concepts of surplus and problems in its measurement. In Part B, major instruments of surplus mobilization have been highlighted. Terms of trade as an instrument of surplus mobilization have been analysed in the third chapter. The fourth chapter shows the trend in market arrivals of major crops. The fifth chapter deals with taxation and expenditure policies resorted to for diverting financial resources. In Part C, one of the concepts of surplus and major instruments of its mobilization have been tested for the state of Punjab. In the end, on the basis of the concept adopted and data employed, major conclusions which have emerged out of my study have been listed. Thus, the study attempts to give an integrated view of the problem in hand.

Acknowledgements

This book has grown out of my doctoral dissertation accepted by the Punjabi University under the title "Mobilization of Agricultural Surpluses in Punjab from 1967-68 to 1981-82". The dissertation was written under the joint supervision of Professor Govind Khanna, a former Head, and Professor J.R. Gupta, the present Head of the Department of Economics at the University. Both of them provided able and constructive guidance and gave the necessary moral support to complete the study. I am indeed grateful to them for their kindness.

The concept of "agricultural surplus" is not free from ambiguity. For providing clarity on its meaning and content, I am beholden to Professor Bhabatosh Datta and the late Professor D.T. Lakdawala who found time to write to me in some detail.

Professor H.K. Manmohan Singh, an Emeritus Professor in the Department and a former Vice-Chanceller of the University, drew my attention to the enhanced importance of the study of the concept of agricultural surplus and the instruments through which this surplus can be mobilized after India entered its newly charted course of economic liberalization and signed the GATT Treaty. He was kind enough to read the entire text twice and to give many valuable suggestions for its improvement. I am deeply indebted to him for all that he has done.

Dr Gulshan Kataria, a Reader in the Department of English, helped in tidying up the manuscript for publication. I must thank him. I am also thankful to Mr Rajesh Kumar for typing the manuscript.

Punjabi University,
Patiala.

VIPLA CHOPRA

PART A

1

Role of Agriculture in Economic Development

INTERRELATIONSHIP between the growth of agriculture and the growth of industry and the contribution that each can make to the other have long interested economists. The interdependence of the agricultural and the non-agricultural sector limits the usefulness of considering the development of either in isolation from the other.

It is essential to recognize that successful industrialization depends upon attainment of an agricultural surplus, and that the pace of industrialization is limited by the rate of agricultural progress. Industrial development and agricultural development are complementary and support each other with respect to inputs as well as outputs.

While rising agricultural productivity and industrial urban development clearly have much to contribute to each other, and hence to overall economic growth, the problem of establishing priorities which faces the development planner is a very difficult one. Recognizing the necessity of choice, economists have fallen into two groups with regard to their judgment as to the relative emphasis which agricultural investment should receive. In the first group are those (like A.E. Kahn, Jacob Viner, and Coale and Hoover) who argue that efforts to increase food supply should receive top priority because of the high demand and great need for additional food or because the highest marginal productivity of capital lies in agriculture.[1] In the second group fall an increasing number of economists (among them Albert Hirschman, Leibenstein, and Higgins) who, while recognizing the need for raising agricultural productivity, conclude that it can be accomplished only by giving top priority to a 'big Push' industrialization programme. Admittedly, there is probably no underdeveloped country which can, at any stage, afford to concentrate all of its investment either on agricultural or on industrial development. In the short run, it is better to concentrate more on agricultural sector and in the long run, when a viable base has been formed, more efforts be diverted to industrialization.

The role of agriculture in the economic development of any country is borne out by the fact that it is the primary sector of the economy which provides the basic ingredients necessary for the existence of mankind. It also provides most of the raw materials which, when transformed into finished products, serve as the basic necessities of the human race. In addition to supplying food, agriculture must provide many of the raw materials essential for industry. It must also generate export surpluses in order to earn foreign exchange which may be further used to finance the import of capital goods and certain kinds of industrial raw material. In addition, agriculture is also a supplier of production factors such as capital and labour.

Bruce F. Johnston and John W. Mellor identify two important relations, which distinguish the agricultural sector in an underdeveloped country and its role in economic growth, that in virtually all underdeveloped countries agriculture is an industry of major proportions, and that secular decline takes place in the size of the agricultural sector as the process of economic growth occurs.[2] Johnston and Mellor further indicate the importance of the process of structural transformation; the size of capital requirements place a great burden on agriculture to provide capital for the expansion of other sectors. In order to fully consider the transfer problem, some understanding of the inter-sectoral relationships that exist between agriculture and industry is necessary.

Johnston and Mellor list five categories of contribution of agriculture to economic development. These are:

(a) Farm products for domestic consumption.

(b) Export of farm products and consequent earnings of foreign exchange.

(c) Transfer of manpower to the industrial sector.

(d) Flow of money into capital formation.

(e) Increased incomes in agriculture as a market for industrial products.

Simon Kuznets, on the other hand, identifies three categories of contribution of agriculture to economic development.[3] They are:-

(a) Product contribution.

(b) Market contribution.

(c) Factor contribution.

By product contribution, he means increase in the total net or gross output of the country or the growth of the product per capita. An increase in the net output of agriculture represents a rise in the output of the country. This type of contribution from agriculture is constituted by the growth of product within the sector itself. This product contribution to the economic growth of a country will be higher, if the share of agriculture in the country's labour force is higher, and the ratio of product per worker in agriculture to that of non-agricultural sector is higher. Secondly, as the economic growth proceeds, and the share of agriculture in the labour force decreases, there will be a continuous decrease in the proportional contribution of agriculture to economic growth.

In the early stages of growth, this market contribution of agriculture to economic growth is larger because at that stage agriculture accounts for a greater share of the net output of the economy. So, the magnitude of the trade with other sectors of the economy will be larger and thus it will have a greater bearing on the economic base of the country. But as the growth proceeds and there is a decrease in the share of agriculture in both product and labour force, there is a tendency towards decline in proportion of market contribution to the total output of the economy. In short, we can say that this market contribution of agriculture is very important in the early stages of growth, but this contribution declines as the growth proceeds apace. In the early stages of growth of many of the developed countries of today, agriculture was an important source of exports and this facilitated the process of modernization. Thus, the contribution of agriculture to exports assumes strategic importance.

The third type of contribution of agriculture to economic growth occurs when there is transference of resources from agriculture to other sectors of the economy.

The market contribution from agriculture is made through the medium of trade with other countries. Kuznets remarks: "Agriculture makes a market contribution to economic growth by (a) purchasing some production items from other sectors at home or abroad; (b) selling some of its product, not only to pay for the purchases listed under (a) but also to purchase consumer goods from other sectors or from abroad, or to dispose of the product in any way other than consumption within the sector. In all these ways, agriculture makes it feasible for other sectors in the economy to merge and grow and for international flows to develop; just as these other sectors and the international flows make it feasible for the agricultural sector to operate more efficiently as a producing unit and use its product more effectively as a consuming unit".[4]

Thus, if agriculture itself grows, it makes product contribution; if it trades with others, it makes a market contribution; and if it transfers resources to other sectors, these resources being productive factors, it makes a factor contribution. These transferred resources can either be capital or labour. There can be compulsory transfer of resources from agriculture through taxation.

Thus development economists have recognized that the performance of the agricultural sector is an important factor in determining the overall success of a particular country's programme for development. More specifically, conventional economics argues that agriculture should serve as a source of food, raw materials, labour and possibly savings for the expansion of the industrial sector. In other words, a net outflow of resources from agriculture to industry should be generated and these resources should be used to promote the rapid expansion of the non-agricultural sector. Agriculture is thought to be the only sector capable of performing such a role since it is usually the largest and the most important sector in the less developed countries.[5]

Similar views have been expressed by Kuznets : "One of the crucial problems of modern economic growth is how to extract from the product of agriculture a surplus for the financing of capital formation necessary for industrial growth without at the same time blighting the growth of agriculture, under conditions where no easy quid pro quo for such surplus is available within the country".[6]

Several economists have strongly criticized the conventional view of the role of agriculture in the development process. For example, Hla Myint has argued that a policy aimed at the extraction of resources from agriculture will cripple the growth potential of agriculture, thus leading to a slow-down in the overall development process. This is due to the fact that the agricultural sectors of most less developed countries require significant resource investments before rapid productivity increases could be expected.[7] Such a net inflow is required, according to Myint, for two basic reasons:—

First, the success of new technologies in food production generally depends on a high standard of irrigation and flood control, and in many less developed countries the provision of these facilities would require very heavy capital investment.

Secondly, in order to promote rapid agricultural expansion, the less developed countries would need to import large quantities of chemical fertilizer. Thus it would seem that a rapid expansion of agricultural production would require a net transfer of resources from the industrial sector, thereby slowing growth. Alternatively, if a less developed society attempts to transfer a net surplus from agriculture, production there would be critically affected thus posing problems for the continued expansion of industry.

Those who emphasize over much on the development of industries claim that higher income is associated with higher degree of industrialization. The rate of return on investment in manufacturing is higher than that in agriculture. Industrialization provides job opportunities and lessens the burden of excessive population on agriculture. Industrialization is also necessary to free the developing countries from the effect of fluctuations in the prices of primary products.

Thus, agriculture and industry both have their own importance for economic development of an underdeveloped country. Though there exists a controversy regarding the impact of inter-sector resource transfers on the development process, Johnston and Mellor have pleaded that net transfer of resources from agriculture to industry can be made without retarding agricultural growth. According to Simon Kuznets, the agricultural sector should transfer to the non-agricultural sector the surplus of investible resources generated in agriculture.

However, there is no a prior reason to expect that at the relevant stage of development, agriculture will possess the capacity to loan or surrender resources. The possibility that the transfer of resources from agriculture may indeed hamper agricultural growth has also been sometimes suggested, for instance, by Oshima (1965), Nicholls (1963), Vakil and Brahmananda (1956)[8]. Ishikawa (1969) has opined explicitly that, at least in the case of centemporary Asian developing countries, significant resource flows into agriculture are likely to be necessary to finance capital intensive investment needed to introduce technical change in agriculture and hence increase agricultural productivity and output.[9]

Similarly, J.W. Mellor, who believes that in the long-run, "the process of economic transformation will proceed more rapidly if a net transfer of income and savings can be made from the agricultural sector to the other sectors of the economy", concedes that "although a relative decline in agriculture and the growth of non-agricultural sector is inevitable in development, it does not follow that maximising the short-run outflow of capital from agriculture will maximize economic development. The development of agriculture can materially contribute to overall economic development and it requires a major inflow of certain forms of capital".[10]

Sudipto Mundle has constructed time-series data for India concerning the transfer of resources for the period 1951-71.[11] Within the study period covered, he identified three phases:

(i) the first half of 1950's when, starting with a net inflow of resources into agriculture, the quantum of such inflow tended to decline;

(ii) the decade from the mid-1950's to mid-1960's, with a rising outflow of resources from agriculture; and

(iii) the later half of the 1960's, when the resource outflow from agriculture recorded a significant decline.

Ashok Mody has also worked out the direction of resource flows between agriculture and non-agriculture in India.[12] He found out a net financial inflow of resources in the agricultural sector through 1950's and 1960's. He further concluded that financial flows into agriculture by way of government expenditure were necessary to create capital-intensive development in agriculture, which in turn, led to a saving potential in this sector which was yet to be tapped.

So, it is evident that there are several dimensions to inter-sector resource flows.

Theoretical literature on the role of agriculture in economic development can be traced as far back as the eighteenth century in the writings of physiocrats in France. The mercantilists had looked upon trade as the most important sector for initiating economic development. The physiocrats argued that the non-agricultural sector was "sterile" as it did not generate economic surplus. Their fundamental proposition was that only agriculture produced an economic surplus or "net product" over the cost of production and that, therefore, the agricultural sector played the most strategic role in economic development. They pointed out that the rate of growth of non-agricultural sector was limited by the growth of the agricultural sector, which in turn flourished most in a system of free competition.[13] So, their general conclusions were that generation of an economic surplus was confined to agriculture and the size of the surplus was determined by the technique of farming or capital intensity of agriculture. They attributed great importance to accumulation of agricultural capital as a pre-condition for the growth of the economy in general.

In the basic models underlying physiocracy and classical economics, the economic surplus generated in the agricultural sector is seen as setting the limit to the process of expansion for the economy as a whole. "This surplus is simply defined as the excess of product which remains after wages and other costs of production have been paid, and is therefore regarded as equal to rent plus profits, which together constitute the society's net disposable income. In physiocratic as well as classical growth models, the manner of utilization of this net product determines the rate and extent of economic development which can be achieved in a country".[14]

Francois Quesnay was the leader and central figure of the physiocratic school. He followed up his analysis to show how the emergence of an economic surplus in agriculture owing to accumulation of capital and technological change would affect other sectors of the economy such as manufacture, trade and commerce, and services which he termed as 'sterile'. From his assumption that an economy's effective demand for marketable output depends on the expenditure of the agricultural surplus, which has a multiplier effect on demand, and his further assumption that the relative size of the agricultural and industrial sectors of the economy depends upon how demand is distributed between these two sectors. He reached his fundamental conclusion that economic development in a country was not possible without agricultural growth, and that the industrial and other sectors of the economy were wholly dependent on the agricultural sector since the demand for manufacture and services depended on the size of the economic surplus which was wholly derived from agriculture.[15]

Adam Smith and other classicals, too, held similar views.[16] Adam Smith, in discussing the natural course of things, said that ". . . the greater part of the capital of every growing society is first directed to agriculture, afterwards to manufactures, and last of all to foreign commerce...." It is the surplus produce of the country only, or whatever is over and above the maintenance of the cultivators, that contributes to the subsistence of the town, which can therefore only increase with the increase of the surplus product."[17]

David Ricardo developed Adam Smith's agriculture model (one-sector model) by introducing the manufacturing sector. Ricardo recognized that, in his two-sector model, the agriculture sector would still be the more important sector as it would set a limit to the growth of the economy as a whole. Ricardo's arguments can be understood with reference to the peculiarity of agriculture where corn appears as both the input and output. It is, therefore, the corn rate of profit in agriculture quite independently of the money rate of profit. In the manufacturing sector, inputs and outputs are heterogeneous; it is, therefore, difficult to obtain a real rate of profit which would be parallel to the corn rate of profit in agriculture. In a competitive model, the money rate of profit earned on capital must be the same in industry and agriculture. But the money rate of profit in agriculture can not be different from the corn rate of profit in the long-term, as the corn rate of profit must determine the money rate. Therefore, the money rate of profit in industry must also depend upon the corn rate of profit in agriculture. The equality in the rate of profit in money terms can be attained as between the two branches only by means of the prices of industrial goods becoming cheaper or dearer than the price of corn. It is this type of reasoning which led Ricardo to conclude that it is the corn rate of profit which determines all other profits in the economy. It is, therefore, quite correct to say that the agricultural sector in Ricardian economics holds the key to our understanding of the process of economic development as a whole.[18]

W.A. Lewis assigned agriculture a significant role in economic development in as much as it provides subsistence to labour in non-agricultural sector and so its growth becomes crucial to development process.[19] According to him, in underdeveloped countries, there is a great pressure of population on land. There is unlimited supply of labour in the rural sector. It is possible that a part of the surplus labour force in the rural areas is not in a state of formal unemployment. These workers are perhaps maintained in the agricultural sector at near subsistence level and participate in many types of seemingly useful agricultural operations. In reality, however, they are in a state of disguised unemployment, as their marginal productivity is zero or negligible due to the pressure of population on agricuture.[20] Now, Lewis argues that it is possible to siphon off the surplus labour, particularly unskilled labour, from agriculture to industry at a constant wage rate which is determined by (though somewhat higher than) the subsistence level of income in the rural sector. In this sense, Lewis, like the classical economists, postulates that the supply of labour to industry in an underdeveloped economy is perfectly elastic at a given wage rate.[21] The transfer of surplus labour from the rural sector cannot reduce agricultural output because its contribution to the marginal product in agriculture is almost zero. If the surplus labour is transferred to industry, it begins to contribute to the marginal product in industry, which is greater than the wage rate required to effect the transfer from agriculture to industry. In this way, the transfer of labour from the rural sector to the industry must increase national output.

Lewis has designed a model of economic development which has been further generalized by Ranis and Fei, and Jorgenson.[22] The former's model ignores agricultural sector altogether, except as a reservoir of labour, while in the later's models the structural interdependence of the agricultural and non-agricultural sector is emphasized. All these models, however, assume the existence of severe disguised unemployment in the agricultural sector.

The Fei-Ranis model depicts the mechanism in which agriculture is considered to be an important source of capital formation for industrial development.[23] Ranis and Fei in their later model (1964) have introduced the net transfer of real sources from agriculture to industry as a central linkage of the development process. They think that it would be the savings of the agriculture sector that constitute the principal source of accumulation during the earlier stages of development while the internal surpluses of the industrial sector are still very limited.

Another model which examines the role of agriculture in economic development is developed by D.W. Jorgenson.[24] Jorgenson asserts even more forcefully than Ranis and Fei that the process of capital formation and economic development cannot proceed smoothly without technological change in the agricultural sector. Only when technological change raises agricultural productivity to a level where the agricultural output is sufficient to feed not only those who remain in agriculture but also the migrating workers from agriculture to industry will the necessary condition for economic transformation be satisfied.

Nevertheless it has to be recognized that the basic concept of development implicit in the entire range of dual economy models of Lewis, Ranis-Fei and Jorgenson variety is the same.

The concept of surplus rural labour population played an important part in the theoretical writings of Ragner Nurkse, W.A. Lewis, H. Leibenstein and P.N. Rosenstein Rodan in the 1950's.[25] Theodore Schultz was one of the first economists to refute the doctrine of disguised unemployment in the sense in which it was used to describe the agricultural situation in the less developed countries.[26]

Morton Paglin[27] supports Schultz's findings regarding the surplus labour hypothesis which is based on extensive data relating to the Farm Management Studies of Indian Agriculture.

He points out that the data offer no conclusive evidence of the existence of zero marginal productivity of labour in Indian agriculture. According to him the available evidence suggests that an increase of hired labour inputs, if combined with the same quantity of other inputs, will lead to larger agricultural output and in particular, there is a definite under-utilization of land on the relatively large holdings in India.

Ragnar Nurkse has suggested a model of resource mobilization in which the process of growth in underdeveloped countries can be made self-financing through the mobilization of saving potential concealed in disguised unemployment in their agricultural sectors.[28]

Shakuntla Mehra[29] has endeavoured to measure disguised unemployment in agriculture in India and defined the concept as follows:

> "The appropriate concept of surplus refers to that work-force as surplus which, with unchanged techniques and organization of farm structure, can be siphoned off without adversely affecting agricultural output."

Thus we see that in whatever manner a particular growth model is framed, the underlying idea remains that agricultural sector must become an object of manipulation for extracting and appropriating surpluses (in the form of reproducible capital, labour force, etc.) for economic development.

Although literature of a general nature on the role of agriculture in economic development is available, the crucial role the agriculture surpluses have played in economic development, though appreciated, has not been specifically examined. In the scheme of inter-sectoral flow in a developing economy, a vital role is assigned to the mobilization of agriculture surplus, first because of its predominance and secondly because it provides wage goods the availability of which at reasonable prices is necessary for raising productivity. Therefore, increasing agricultural production is of paramount importance to capital accumulation. Resource mobilization is the decisive determinant of the process of capital formation. Resources are the funds for investment. The technique of resource creation, mobilization and investment is the dynamic know-how which moves the wheels of planning and growth in an economy.

The technique of resource mobilization has a two-fold objective of ensuring

(a) the total pool of resources, and

(b) an increasing part of the additions to the pool being channelled into investment.

The dominant issue, therefore, is how available resources can effectively be mobilized and used in the best possible manner to augment the rate of capital formation. The problem is one of creation and mobilization of investible surpluses. We have first to generate resources and then to mobilize them into investment channels.

All the resources required need not be raised from internal sources alone. A country may depend, to some extent, on external resources which are mainly available by way of loans and grants. Even advanced countries borrowed a good deal from other countries when they initiated development plans. But, in general, and in the long run, a developing country will have to depend on its own resources; after all, the external loans will have to be repaid. The next problem which arises is with regard to the choice of sectors from which surpluses are to be raised and to see that resources so mobilized are not wasted away. The surpluses generated in the industrial sector are already being mobilized albeit insufficiently. There is considerable uncertainty about the inflow and adequacy of external resources because they depend on a number of political factors. In the circumstances, agriculture is the only sector wherein surpluses can be generated and mobilized. Also, a major part of the national income in an underdeveloped country originates in the agricultural sector, and therefore, it should not only generate surplus and finance its own investment and capital formation but also help the non-farm sector. In the agricultural sector, a large reservoir of under-utilized labour force exists and the land is not fully exploited. The surplus labour generated in agriculture should effectively be mobilized for development needs.

Next, it is pleaded that though the creation of investible surpluses is easy in agriculture, their direct mobilization for productive purposes is difficult. The problem is not merely to raise additional resources but to raise them in a manner reasonably consistent with the commitment to reducing of inequalities and minimizing of the burden placed on the poorer sections of the people.

In most of the countries, the channelling of agricultural surpluses for economic development was responsible for their take-off. The beginning of take-off is usually traced to a particular stimulus. This stimulus may take the form of political revolution which affects directly the balance of social power and effective values, the character of economic institutions, the pattern of investment outlays, etc. The examples of Japan since 1868, U.S.S.R. since 1917 and China since 1948 have proved how agriculture plays a dynamic role in economic development.

Japan was the first Asian country which despite its traditional form of agriculture, primitive methods of cultivation and very small size of landholdings, succeeded in bringing a striking phase of agricultural development.

In Japan a substantial increase in agricultural production was attained by the adoption of increased irrigation facilities, improved seeds, advanced knowledge, etc. Thus the dynamic nature of the Japanese society and great efforts made to enhance the agricultural production yielded quick results and it was due to this that the required surpluses from the agricultural sector were siphoned off, in an indirect way, to other areas by the imposition of heavy land tax which amounted to 63.7 per cent of the aggregate tax yield in 1868, 93.2 per cent in 1873 and 83.2 per cent in 1877. Many alternatives to land tax have, however, emerged recently.

In the U.S.S.R., initially inadequate agricultural production was a major impediment in the process of industrialization, but the enforcement of collectivization largely changed the picture. The basic reasons for the introduction of collectivization were political rather than economic.

The Soviet Government wanted to set up a socialist society and nationalize all lands. In so far as economic reasons were concerned, the transition of the Soviet villages to large agricultural farms meant a great revolution in economic relations in the entire way of life of the peasantry. Collectivization put an end for ever to the exploitation of the peasants by large farmers and Kulaks. Also, all the advantages of large-scale farming could be reaped by the introduction of collective farms.

In China, in addition to the taxes payable in kind, the peasants were bound to sell large quantities of cereals and certain other agricultural goods to the state. This was a form of disguised taxation.

Thus, it can be maintained on the basis of historical evidence that the strength and pace of industrial growth of any nation depend primarily on the strength of its agricultural sector. No country has moved from chronic stagnation into the take-off stage of economic development without first achieving a breakthrough in agricultural productivity. More specifically, conventional economists argue that agriculture should serve as a source of food, raw materials, labour and possibly savings for the expansion of the industrial sector. In other words, a net outflow of resources from agriculture to industry should be generated and used to promote rapid expansion of non-agricultural sector. Agriculture is thought to be the only sector capable of performing such a role since it is usually the largest and most important sector in the less developed countries.[30]

REFERENCES

1. Harvey Leibenstein, *Economic Backwardness and Economic Growth,* (New York, John Willey, 1957), pp. 261-262.
2. Bruce F. Johnston and John W. Mellor, "The Role of Agriculture in Economic Development", *American Economic Review,* (Vol 51,

No. 4, September, 1961), p. 566.

3. Simon Kuznets, "Economic Growth and the Contribution of Agriculture: Notes on Measurements", in Carl, K. Eicher and Lawrence W. Witt, (ed.), *Agriculture in Economic Development,* (New York, McGraw Hill Book Company, 1964), pp. 102-119.

4. *Ibid.*

5. Bruce F. Johnston and John W. Mellor, *op. cit.,* pp. 566-593.

6. Simon Kuznets, *op.cit.,* p. 115.

7. As quoted in Richard Grabowski and Bong Joon Yoon, "Intersectoral Resource Flows and Economic Development: The Case of India", *Indian Journal of Agricultural Economics,* (October-December, 1982), p. 503.

8. As quoted in Ashok Mody, "Resource Flows between Agriculture and Non-agriculture in India, 1950-1970", *Economic and Political Weekly,* (Annual Number, March, 1981), p. 425.

9. S. Ishikawa, *Economic Development in Asian Perspective,* (Tokyo, The Institute of Economic Research, Histotsubashy University, 1967).

10. As quoted in Ashok Mody, *op.cit.,* p. 425.

11. Sudipto Mundle, *Surplus Flows and Growth Imbalances: The Inter-Sectoral Flow of Real Resources in India 1951-1971,* (New Delhi, Allied Publishers Private Limited, 1981).

12. Ashok Mody, *op.cit.*

13. J.J. Spengler, "Mercantilist and Physiocratic Growth Theory", in Best F.Hoselitez (ed.), *Theories of Economic Growth,* (1960), pp. 54-56.

14. R.N. Ghosh, *Agriculture in Economic Development: With Special Reference to Punjab,* (New Delhi, Vikas Publishing House, Pvt. Ltd., 1977), p. 10.

15. *Ibid.,* p. 5.

16. Adam Smith, *An Inquiry into the Nature and Causes of the Wealth of Nations,* edited by Edwin Cannan (New York, The Modern Library, 1937), p. 291.

17. *Ibid.*

18. N. Kaldor, *Alternative Theories of Distribution: Review of Economic Studies,* (Vol. 23, 1955-56).

19. W.A. Lewis, "Economic Development with Unlimited Supplies of Labour", *The Manchester School of Economic and Social Studies,* (Vol. 22, May 1954), pp. 131-191.
20. R.N. Ghosh, *op.cit.,* pp. 11-12.
21. W.A.Lewis, *op.cit.*
22. G. Ranis and C.H. Fei, "A Theory of Economic Development", *American Economic Review,* (September, 1961); D.W. Jorgenson, "The Development of a Dual Economy", *Economic Journal,* (June, 1961); "Surplus Agricultural Labour and the Development of a Dual Economy", *Oxford Economic Papers,* (November, 1967).
23. Ranis Gustav and C.H.Fei, *Development of Labour Surplus Economy: Theory and Policy,* (Home Wood III, Irwin, 1964).
24. Dale W. Jorgenson, "The Development of Dual Economy", *Economic Journal,* (Vol. LXXI, June, 1961), pp. 309-334.
25. (a) Ragnar Nurkse, *Problems of Capital Formation in Underdeveloped Countries,* (Delhi, Oxford University Press, 1953).
    (b) W. Arthur Lewis, *The Theory of Economic Growth,* (London, George Allen and Unwin, 1960).
    (c) Harvey Leibenstein, *op.cit.*
    (d) P.N. Rosenstein - Rodan, "Disguised Unemployment and Underemployment in Agriculture", *Monthly Bulletin of Agricultural Economics and Statistics,* (Vol. 6, Rome: F.A.O., July-August, 1957).
26. Theodore W. Schultz, *Transforming Traditional Agriculture,* (New Heaven, Yale University Press, 1964).
27. M. Paglin: "Surplus Agricultural Labour and Development Facts and Figures", *American Economic Review,* (September, 1965).
28. R. Nurkse, *op. cit.*
29. S. Mehra, "Surplus Labour in Indian Agriculture", *Indian Economic Review,* (N.S., April, 1966).
30. Bruce F. Johnston and John W. Mellor, *op.cit.,* pp. 566-593.

2

Concept of 'Surplus' and its Measurement Problems

'SURPLUS' has been defined differently by different authors, and there does not exist any single common definition of it. Paul Baran, Raja J. Chelliah, Nichlos Kaldor, etc. are some of those who have given their version of the concept. Paul Baran (1957), for instance, distinguishes between actual economic surplus and potential economic surplus.[1] Actual economic surplus is "the difference between society's actual current output and its actual current consumption". It is, thus identical with current saving or accumulation, and finds its embodiment in assets of various kinds added to society's wealth, productive facilities and equipment, inventories, foreign balances and gold hoards. Actual economic surplus has been generated in all socio-economic systems and while its size and structure have markedly differed from one phase of development to another, its existence has been observed in nearly all recorded history. Potential economic surplus is the difference between the output that could be produced in a given natural and technological environment with the help of employable productive resources, and what might be regarded as essential consumption. It is, of course, impossible to define precisely the term "essential consumption". It is not fixed for all times nor is it the same for all countries and groups, nevertheless, for a given society, at a given time, it is possible to have a rough idea of the essential consumption required in its quantitative and qualitative aspects. Its realization pre-supposes a more or less drastic reorganization of the production and distribution of social output and implies far-reaching changes in the structure of society. It appears under four headings. One is society's excess consumption; the second is the output lost to society through the existence of unproductive workers; the third is the output lost because of the irrational and wasteful organization of the existing productive apparatus; and the fourth is the output foregone owing to the existence of unemployment caused primarily by the anarchy of capitalist production and the deficiency of effective demand. The identification and measurement of these four forms of the potential economic surplus runs into some obstacles.[2]

Further, the character of a civilization and its future progress depend on the purposes for which and the manner in which the surplus is utilized. This surplus can be used for 'an unproductive consumption' or for 'unproductive investment' or for 'productive investment'. Economic progress requires that in the initial stages, at any rate, a high proportion of this surplus be channelled into productive investment. Paul Baran points out that in an agrarian country like India, a great part of the surplus can originate in the agricultural sector and is appropriated by landowners, money-lenders and merchants. What is required is a comprehensive mobilization of the economic surplus currently generated in the economy.

Raja J. Chelliah, following Paul Baran, speaks of 'economic surplus' which, in his view, goes waste or at least to 'unproductive consumption' or 'unproductive investment', but which, if mobilized and harnessed to the task of development, would open the door to prosperity and wealth. "Civilization", he says, "is made possible for any society or nation when its economic system begins to generate a surplus over essential consumption. The character of a civilization and its future progress depend on the purpose for which and the manner in which the surplus is utilized".[3]

Howsoever destitute a nation might be on the whole, there are areas where such surpluses are found and it is the task of the fiscal policy to mop up this surplus and to channel it along ways which will be productive of wealth.

Nicholas Kaldor has given a different version of the concept of economic surplus.[4] To him, economic surplus is not represented by the excess of production over the minimum subsistence needs of the population. He argues that "it would be more correct to say that the taxation potential of a country depends on the excess of its actual consumption over the minimum consumption of the population".[5] If existing savings are already directed into productive channels, then it is true that further taxation potential depends on the excess of the country's actual consumption over the minimum required essential consumption. But if that is not so, the potential investment in output resulting from a better utilization of existing savings should also be considered.

H.R. Wagstaff defines economic surplus as the difference between what a society produces and the cost of producing it.[6] The size of the surplus is an index of productivity and wealth of how much freedom a society has to accomplish whatever goals it may set for itself. The composition (i.e. absorption) of the surplus shows how it uses that freedom.

So far the concept of surplus defined as economic surplus has been discussed. Now an attempt is made to give different versions of the concept of 'agricultural surplus'. Although the role of agricultural surplus has been strongly emphasized in the writings of many economists[7] and in the history of economic development of many countries like Japan, China, the USSR and Canada,[8] there does not exist any single common definition of the concept.

W.H. Nicholls defined agricultural surplus as the physical amount by which, in any given country, total food production exceeds the total food consumption of the agricultural population. He has built a partial analytical model which gives greater precision to the concept of agricultural surplus. He concludes that, "until underdeveloped countries succeed in achieving and sustaining (either through domestic production or imports) a reliable food surplus, they have not fulfilled the fundamental pre-condition for economic development".[9]

V. Rajagopalan divided the path of development into three phases on the basis of the behaviour of total and average agricultural surplus.[10] Total agricultural surplus is the difference between total output and total consumption in agriculture. Average agricultural surplus is derived from total agricultural surplus when surplus labour moves out of agriculture. Total agricultural surplus increases till marginal productivity of labour becomes positive. This is the first phase. As labour migrates further, total agricultural surplus with given level of productivity contracts and affects adversely the terms of trade for non-farm sector. This phase is the scarcity phase which extends to a point, termed as commercialization point, at which marginal productivity equals institutional wages. From this point onwards, the allocation process of labour is guided by marginal equilibrium.

According to Sen Bandhudas, the concept of 'agricultural surplus' has been frequently used in literature to emphasize the product contribution of agriculture in the process of development of the non-farm sector.[11] To him, 'agricultural surplus' also represents potential capital, or loanable funds for the acquisition of capital, a part or all of which can be utilized for the initial investment in the non-agricultural sector. Assuming there is a farm product surplus in the first place, over and above the subsistence requirements of the agricultural sector, part of it becomes savings and is lent to the non-farm sector for productive investment; part of it can be taxed away for financing growth of the non-agricultural sector. The existence of an agricultural surplus and its diversion to the non-farm sector thus becomes crucial to economic development.

M.V. George and A.J. Singh, while emphasizing the role of agriculture, conclude that agriculture has a vital role to play in setting the pace for economic development, both as a supplier of physical surpluses in the form of wage goods and raw materials and economic surpluses in the form of savings for investment in the industrial sector.[12]

Peter J. Lloyd presents a single two-sector model which clearly differentiates among three concepts of an agricultural surplus — a surplus of food production over the consumption in the agricultural sector (Z^1), saving out of agricultural income (Z^2), and a surplus of domestic production over domestic absorption of the output of this sector which is available for export (Z^3), and considers the role of these surpluses in the growth of an economy.[13]

T.J. Byres spells out briefly the kind of resource flow that is necessary in the 'early years of industrialization' (or the period of primitive accumulation) when the rate of industrial growth is critically dependent upon the transfer of an agricultural surplus.[14] He further divides the agricultural surplus into two main parts; a real surplus and a financial surplus. The real surplus (real because it is physical in its manifestation) has two components, food and raw materials. Food is crucial for the whole of the industrial sector since it is the wage-good par excellence. If the marketed surplus of food is not forthcoming both in sufficient quantity and favourable terms, industrialization will be held back. Raw materials from agriculture are essential for key industries like textiles and for other agro-based industries, which are important in the early years of industrialization as earners of foreign exchange, employers of labour and producers of consumer goods.

The other component of agricultural surplus, namely, financial surplus represents a command over resources which can be transferred from the agricultural to the non-agricultural sector. The difference between a large and a modest investment rate outside agriculture will depend on the financial surplus or, in other words, on the extent to which agriculture relinquishes its command over real resources. The aim is to secure the maximum marginal rate of saving in the agricultural sector and acquire these savings in order to use them for financing capital formation in the industrial sector. Again, movements in the marketed surplus are important.

At the 35th Annual Conference of the Indian Society of Agricultural Economics, a large number of papers on Mobilization of Rural Surpluses for Development were presented.[15] The major issues highlighted in these papers were:

(1) Definitional issue.

(2) Problems of estimation of rural surpluses.

(3) Problems of mobilization of rural surpluses.

As far as (1) is concerned, even in these papers, the concept of rural surplus has been defined differently by different authors. Rural surpluses can be classified into two groups viz., output surpluses and input surpluses. Even the concept of output surplus does not have the same meaning in all the papers.

In some papers, output surplus may mean production surplus or technological surplus. In the words it is the difference between output and input. But estimation of production surplus is difficult due to the problem of aggregation. Most of the papers deal with other two types of surplus, namely financial surplus and marketable surplus. For instance, Ram Kumar, M.L. Sharma and C.S. Sisodia define surplus as excess of output over total expenditure.[16] Jagannath Rao, R. Pawar and Vijay B. Patil's study also accepts the same definition.[17] P.C. Shukla and B.K. Mishra's study estimates the profit from farming by deducting the value of family labour and interest on capital investment from the net farm income.[18] S.P. Sinha, B.N.Verma and D.K. Sinha, in their study, estimated marketed surplus of foodgrains.[19]

The other type of surplus, namely input surplus is taken as the excess of supply of inputs in the rural sector over their sectoral use. The availability of excess capacity in the rural sector, and the availability of execes labour over and above the required magnitude may give rise to the capital surpluses and labour surpluses, respectively. Surplus labour is defined as the difference between the labour supply and its utilization. Almost all the studies present time-unit availability of surplus labour. However, utilization of labour supply has a different coverage in different studies. P.K. Chatterjee and Shibdas Bannerjee considered only adult male labour supply.[20] V.K. Pandey, S.L. Shah and A.K.Singh computed total working units by multiplying the male members in 15-59 age group by 300 working days and the female members in the same age group by 150 working days.[21]

Utilization refers to the peak season. Peak month work-load per family farm worker is considered to be the quantity of labour that cannot be dispensed with throughout the year without bringing about any major organizational changes and perhaps decrease in total output. Ashok K. Mitra defined labour surplus as the difference of actual supply of labour and the minimum labour requirement.[22]

V.T. Raju regards unemployment of workers in the peak season, in West Godavari District, as indicator of the existence of surplus labour.[23]

M.L. Jhingan divides agricutural surpluses into two parts: real surpluses and financial surpluses.[24] The real surpluses have two components, food and raw materials, which are important as the industry's working capital. They are expressed in physical terms as a relation between production and marketed surplus. The financial surpluses represent a command over resources which can be transferred to the industrial sector.

B.L. Mishra, V.P. Shukla and D.K. Marothia identified two types of farm surpluses, namely technological surplus and investible surplus.[25] According to them, technological surplus is the difference between total output and total input and investible surplus is the difference between income and expenditure at the family level. These surpluses were identified in relation to the size of farms and level of farm technology.

According to D.T. Lakdawala, the phrase 'mobilization of agricultural surplus' is used in many ways but the general implication of the phrase is the investment surplus that remains after the agriculturists have consumed according to the usual habits.[26]

Bhabatosh Datta suggested that the problem of mobilization of surpluses can be tackled in two ways.[27] Firstly, the physical agricultural surplus which is necessary for sustaining non-agricultural products can be examined. The most important is the foodgrains surplus needed to feed the non-food producing workers and all others. For this the marketed surplus, the marketable surplus, the surplus over 'necessary' consumption have to be estimated. In the case of non-food crops, where self-consumption may be nil or small, practically the whole output is a surplus in this sense. Mobilization here could be through the market forces and/or official procurement.

Alternatively, savings of agricultural producers can be examined. The physical surplus problem and the savings problem are sometimes linked, but are not always necessarily so. A cultivator's saving (income minus total consumption expenditure) may be zero or even negative, but he may still be able to provide an output surplus over his consumption of that output. Mobilization would mean the provision of institutions and attractive financial assets within easy reach, or taxation that makes a draft on rural savings.

Thus, surplus has been interpreted in different ways. At the same time, it is also not easy to measure the surplus. Its measurement can pose many difficult problems depending on which of the many possible concepts one adopts. Theoretically, some of the concepts may sound good, but practically it may be quite difficult to quantify them. The problems of aggregation, construction of index number, valuation of self-employed labour, etc. are some of them. However, in spite of these limitations, a modest attempt has been made in the present study to measure the magnitude of inter-sector and intra-sector potential surpluses using different approximations in later part of the book.

In spite of different versions of the concept of surplus, there is no doubt about the fact that economic surplus has played a significant role in the planned economic development of India also as it has in the case of Japan, China, Canada, etc.

Role of Economic Surplus in the Planned Economic Development of India

The whole future of planning in India depends, to a considerable extent, on implementing and formulating of suitable policies for mopping up surpluses for purposes of development planning. Economic planning, launched within the framework of democracy, aims at promoting rapid and balanced economic development which is a complicated process.

India has embarked upon a programme of planned economic development since the beginning of the First Five-Year Plan. This has tended to transform the structure of the economy and build up the basic foundation of economic development. The main strategy of the First Plan was connected with the acceleration of the development potential of the agricultural sector so as to facilitate the growth of industries in later years. The First Plan stated: "Without a substantial increase in the production of food and raw materials needed for industry, it would be impossible to sustain a higher tempo of industrial development. In a developing economy with low yields in agriculture, there is, of course, no conflict between agricultural and industrial development. The two are complementary."[28]

The Second Plan made a definite departure from the strategy of balanced sectoral growth. This plan was based on Prof. Mahalanobis model which was based on extraordinary technique of "planning with unbalanced growth". This technique emphasizes the fact that, during the planning period, investment will grow at a higher rate than income; and income, at a higher rate than consumption, so that there will be a process of unbalanced development. The technique directly takes us to the problem of generation of economic surplus. If we rule out considerable amount of capital imports, the main source from which the bulk of the investment in "capital-goods heavy industries" would come is the economic surplus generated by the economic system during the planning period.

The extraction of economic surplus from the economy for the development of heavy industries was done in an outstanding manner by the Russian Planners. They were the first to adopt this technique in a crude form. In Russia, during the planning period, investment grew at a faster rate than consumption. The Russians comparatively neglected consumer goods and over-emphasized heavy industries. They kept consumption at the "rock bottom" level throughout the planning period. For the sake of achieving accelerated growth, the surplus generated by the capital goods industries was reinvested for the further expansion and development of these industries, causing thereby privation and misery to the Russian people. But what the Russians did under a totalitarian set-up is almost impossible in a democratic country like India. Lowering of consumption standard would be an unsound proposition in an underdeveloped country like India because the standard of living of our people is already extremely low, and there is consequently very little scope for depressing it further. The Planning Commission of India has not completely neglected the problem of increasing consumption goods production in the course of the Five-Year Plans. Thus we find that though the Indian planning process has the "unbalanced growth technique" as its main building block, it does not go to such extremes as the Russian planners did in the initial and subsequent periods of planning. In India's Second Five-Year Plan, cottage and household industries were emphasized upon side by side with the heavy producer goods industries. Further, in a democratic country, the mopping up of economic surplus can be successful if people are sufficiently patriotic-minded and realise the urgency of the situation so that there is minimum political resistance to the fiscal-cum-budgetary policies of the government introduced for this purpose. The surplus should be systematically increased, carefully husbanded and properly utilized by means of well co-ordinated, centralized planning.

The development strategy with its emphasis on heavy industries proved to be a great success in the initial phase of planned development. During the Second Plan period, both saving and investment rates rose considerably and output targets were nearly achieved. Further, the country managed to develop a heavy industry complex. During the Third Plan period, however, the development process ran into serious difficulties. During the second half of the 1960's, since the excess demand generated through a high rate of public investment could not be matched with the supply of foodgrains and other consumer goods, an inflationary situation developed. The faith in the development strategy, as defined in the Mahalanobis model, was shaken and a plan holiday was declared for three years.

When the long-term planning was resumed in 1969, the basic framework of the Mahalanobis strategy was resumed. In the Fourth Plan, the objective of self-reliance was not given up, but the main emphasis was shifted to rapid economic growth. Therefore, not only quick-yielding projects were preferred in each economic sector, but light industry was also favoured at the expense of heavy industry. This departure was probably induced by the rapid growth of population which was exercising pressure for increasing the supply of foodgrains and other consumer goods.

The draft Five-Year Plan 1978-83, which the Janata Government adopted, stated a new development strategy. There was a clear shift in the strategy of planning when the Fifth Five-Year Plan was terminated before its period was over.

The investment pattern under the Sixth Plan (1980-85) was not in conformity with the Mahalanobis strategy. The heavy industries were denied the priority they deserved. The Seventh Plan strategy of development stressed the need for developing wage goods sector. This strategy was a variant of what is now known as Agricultural Development-Led Growth (ADLG) strategy. Thus the strategy which enabled the country to step up the rate of economic growth during the eighties pushed the economy towards economic crisis. The crisis began in 1990-91 and the year 1991-92 turned out to be an exceptionally difficult year for the economy with the deepening of the crisis. The government decided to introduce substantial reforms and adopted a new development strategy. The new approach involved four major policy initiatives, (i) fiscal correction, (ii) trade policy reforms, (iii) industrial policy reforms, and (iv) the public sector reforms to improve performance. These policy measures constituted the new development strategy.

Thus, in the end, we can conclude that inspite of different versions of the concept of economic surplus, there is no doubt about the fact that economic surplus has played a crucial role in the economic development of many countries.

REFERENCES

1. Paul Baran, *The Political Economy of Growth,* (New York, Monthly Review Press, 1957), pp. 22-23.
2. R.J. Chelliah, *Fiscal Policy in Underdeveloped Countries,* (London, George Allen and Unwin, 1960), p. 65.
3. *Ibid.,* p. 65.
4. Nicholas Kaldor, "The Role of Taxation in Economic Development", in E.A.G. Robinson (ed.) *Problems in Economic Development,* (London, Macmillan and Co. Ltd., 1965), p. 172.
5. *Ibid.*
6. H.R. Wagstaff, "The Economic Surplus of Agriculture in the United Kingdom", *Journal of Agricultural Economics,* (Vol. XXIII, No. 3, September, 1972), p. 233.
7. (a) S.Kuznets, "Economic Growth and the Contribution of Agriculture: Notes on Measurements", in Carl K. Eicher and Lawrence W. Witt (ed.), *Agriculture in Economic Development,* (New York, McGraw Hill Book Company, 1964), pp. 102-119.
   (b) Bruce F. Johnston and John W. Mellor, "The Role of Agriculture in Economic Development," *American Economic Review,* (Vol. 51, No. 4, September 1961).
   (c) W.A. Lewis, "Economic Development with Unlimited Supplies of Labour", *The Manchester School of Economic and Social Studies,* (Vol. 22, May 1954), pp. 131-191.
8. (a) Thomas C. Smith, *op.cit.*
   (b) Kazurhi Ohkawa and Henry Rosovsky, "The Role of Agriculture in Modern Japanese Economic Development", *Economic Development and Cultural Change,* (Vol. IX, October, 1960).
   (c) Verson W. Yorgasen, "Agriculture in Economic Development: The Competitive Approach Versus Soviet Control", *Canadian Journal of Agricultural Economics,* (Vol. 20, No.1, February 1972), pp. 51-62.
9. William H. Nicholls, "An Agricultural Surplus as a Factor in Economic Development", *Journal of Political Economy,* (Vol. 71, No.1, Feb. 1963), pp. 1-29.
10. V. Rajagopalan, "Some Aspects of Economic Growth in Overpopulated Countries", *Indian Journal of Agricultural Economics,* (Vol. XXII, No. 4, Oct.-Dec. 1967), p. 82.

11. Sen Bandhudas, "The Role of Agriculture's Contributions in the Theory of Economic Growth in Over-populated Countries", *Indian Journal of Agricultural Economics,* (Vol. XXII, No. 4, October-December 1967), p. 92.

12. M.V. George and A.J. Singh, "Role of Agriculture and Strategy for Agricultural Development in Over-populated Countries", *Indian Journal of Agricultural Economics,* (Vol. XXII, No. 4, October-December 1967), p. 102.

13. Peter J. Lloyd, "The Role of 'Agricultural Surpluses' in Economic Development", *The Developing Economies,* (Vol. 8, No. 1-4, March 1970), pp. 39-51.

14. T.J. Byres, "Land Reform, Industrialization and the Marketed Surplus in India: An Essay on the Power of Rural Bias", in David Lehmann (ed.) *Agrarian Reformism Studies of Peru, Chile, China and India,* (London, Faber and Faber Ltd. 1974), pp. 224-225.

15. *Indian Journal of Agricultural Economics,* (Vol. XXX, No. 3, July-September 1975), pp. 1-82.

16. A. Ram Kumar, M.L. Sharma and G.S. Sisodia, "Mobilization of Rural Surplus - A Study of Savings in Rural Hissar", *Ibid.,* pp. 16-25.

17. Jagannath Rao, R. Pawar and Vijay B. Patil, "Measurement of Rural Surpluses at the Micro Level in the Sugar Factory Areas of the Maharashtra State", *Ibid.,* pp. 10-15.

18. P.C. Shukla and B.K. Mishra, "Technological Impact and Saving Potential of Farm Families (A Study of Rai Bareli District)", *Ibid.,* p. 58.

19. S.P. Sinha, B.N. Verma and D.K. Sinha, "A Study of Marketed Surplus, Scale Elasticity of Surplus and Prospect of Mobilizing Surplus in North Bihar, Bahadurpur Block, District Darbhanga", *Ibid.,* pp. 26-30.

20. P.K. Chatterjee, and Shibdas Bannerjee, "Surplus Labour in West Bengal's Agriculture: A Note", *Ibid.,* pp. 60-61.

21. V.K. Pandey, S.L. Shah and A.K. Singh, "Surplus Farm Family, Labour in Uttar Pradesh and Its Mobilization for Economic Development", *Ibid.,* pp. 37-43.

22. Ashok K. Mitra, "Estimation of Surplus Taxes in Agriculture and Problems in Mobilization", *Ibid.,* pp. 31-37.

23. V.T. Raju, "Study of Labour Surplus in West Godavari District", *Ibid.*, p. 59.
24. M.L. Jhingan, "Surpluses Pertaining since the Green Revolution and their Contribution to Industrialization - A Study of Punjab", *Ibid.*, p. 56.
25. B.L. Mishra, V.P. Shukla and D.K. Marothia, "Technological and Investible Surpluses on Tendukheda Farms, Madhya Pradesh", *Ibid.*, p. 57.
26. Through Private Correspondence.
27. *Ibid.*
28. Government of India, Planning Commission: *First Five-Year Plan,* (p. 44).

PART B

3

Terms of Trade

TERMS of trade are considered to be one of the important instruments of mobilization of surplus. By regulating terms of trade against the agricultural sector, surplus of this sector can be mobilized to the non-agricultural sector and vice versa. In other words, relative prices of agricultural and non-agricultural commodities are useful signs of indicating the trends of resource flow between these two sectors via terms of trade. Further, changes in terms of trade have enormous potential of affecting the allocation of resources between sectors, profitability of investment in different sectors, the distribution of national income and the growth of savings and investment and thus the rate of growth of an economy.

Changes in terms of trade alter the profitability of various sectors in the economy and as profit is the guiding motive of production, it can powerfully affect the flow of resources from one sector to another. If the prices of products of one sector in terms of the prices of products of the other increase, the profitability in the other sector declines. So, resources will flow out from the latter into the former sector. Thus, there will be diversion of resources, which will affect the pace of growth of the two sectors as well as the overall economic growth.

Changes in terms of trade not only affect economic development directly, but affect it indirectly, too, through their effect on the rate of capital formation. Changes in terms of trade will raise the level of savings in that sector, in favour of which terms of trade have moved, assuming that savings are a function of income. On the other hand, in the other sector, the level of savings and investment will be reduced. As the marginal propensity to save and invest is different in different sectors of the economy, the effect of shifting terms of trade will depend on whether terms of trade have moved in favour of the sector having high marginal propensity to save and invest or not. If it so happens, there will be a net addition to the savings fund of the economy.

Changes in terms of trade redistribute income not only between different sectors of the economy but also between different income groups within a sector. If the prices of one sector's product rise in terms of those of the other sector, this sector will gain both as a buyer and a seller so that the income of the sector will increase. Similarly, different income groups will be affected differently, depending upon how much they sell to the other sector and how much they purchase from it. Thus the income inequality may be narrowed or widened. Changes in terms of trade also affect the factoral distribution. Terms of trade affect not only the shares of factors of production in national income but also the mobility of factors of production. Changes in domestic terms of trade may affect the revenue of the government, too; the relative prices may cause re-distribution of income from a high tax paying community to low tax paying community, thereby reducing the resources of the government. Thus, movement in domestic terms of trade has far-reaching effects and its importance in the process of economic transition has been well realized recently by W.A. Lewis, R.S. Eckaus, Georgescu-Roegen, D.W. Jorgenson, Johnston-Mellor and Ranis and Fei.[1]

There are various concepts of terms of trade, the use of which may lead to different conclusions. The loss or gain to a particular sector from changes in the terms of trade will depend, in a decisive way, on which concept we are using. Jacob Viner used the concept of 'terms of trade' for the first time in the context of theories of international trade to describe the phenomenon of changing ratios of the prices of exports of a country to the prices of its imports.[2]

Various concepts like commodity terms of trade or net barter terms of trade, income terms of trade, single factoral and double factoral terms of trade etc. have been used in the theory of international trade.[3] These concepts may serve a similar purpose in a closed economy to show the distribution of gains through shifts in terms of trade.

The usual method to determine the sectoral terms of trade is to study the relative movements in the prices of agricultural and non-agricultural goods with reference to a base year. In a two-sector economy, it may be defined as the ratio of index of agricultural prices to the index of industrial prices with reference to a common base year in which indices of both prices are equated to 100. It may be expressed as:

$$N = P_A / P_I$$

That is to say, this ratio denotes the relationship between the prices of both the sectors,

where N = Net barter terms of trade

P_A = Index of agricultural prices

P_I = Index of industrial prices.

An increase in the ratios P_A / P_I means a rise in the prices of agricultural products in terms of industrial products.

Another concept which is used is income terms of trade, which may be defined as :

$$I = N.Q_A$$

where I = Income terms of trade

N = Commodity terms of trade

Q_A = Value of sales of the agricultural sector.

The commodity terms of trade cannot be an appropriate measure of increased or decreased welfare of a sector. The welfare of a sector will also depend upon the changes in the productivity of the inputs used in that sector i.e. on the technological change in the sector.

Jacob Viner introduced the concept of factoral terms of trade which, in the case of a closed economy can be modified as:[4]

$S = NZ_A$

where S = Factoral terms of trade

N = Commodity terms of trade

Z_A = Index of productivity in the agricultural sector.

A rise in the single factoral terms of trade indicates increased welfare of the agricultural sector, meaning thereby that the real earnings of the factors employed in the agricultural sector have increased.

If productivity in both the sectors is taken into account, we shall have double factoral terms of trade, which can be expressed as :

$$D = \frac{N Z_A}{Z_I}$$

where D = Double factoral terms of trade

N = Net barter terms of trade

Z_A = Index of productivity of the agricultural sector

Z_I = Index of productivity of the industrial sector.

A rise in D means that a unit of factor embodied in the agricultural product exchanges for more units of factors embodied in the industrial product. While analysing the gains from inter-sectoral exchange, productivity of both the sectors must be taken into account. In this respect, double factoral terms of trade are a better measure than the single factoral terms of trade.

The commodity terms of trade and double factoral terms of trade will amount to the same thing, if the technical co-efficients for the two products remain the same, or, there are constant returns to scale in both the sectors.

Hence, a better measure of whether the welfare of the agricultural sector has increased or decreased in the process of economic growth will be the farmer's terms of trade. It may be defined as the ratio between agricultural and non-agricultural prices. That is to say, this ratio denotes the relationship between the prices of both the sectors. Perhaps, one of the ways of mobilizing agricultural surpluses in a country like India is to deliberately fashion the price policy in such a way that the terms of trade move against agriculture so that for realising the same money income the total quantum of marketed surplus has to be increased.

No one concept is sufficient to explain the gains from the changes in terms of trade in inter-sectoral exchange. All the concepts suffer from their own limitations. The choice of a particular concept of the terms of trade is a difficult problem. Mostly, commodity terms of trade with a common base year are used in practice. However, the economic welfare or the income of a sector in the sectoral exchange is not affected by the prices of all the commodities produced in the two sectors but by the prices of only those commodities which actually enter into exchange i.e. which are actually bought and sold. The prosperity of the agricultural sector depends not only on the prices of the products of this sector, but also upon the prices of the products of the other sectors as economic and overall welfare is a relative thing. "The real return that he (the farmer) gets does not depend upon the prices he obtains for his produce; it depends as much upon the prices, in turn, he has to pay for what he buys. If any increase in food prices raises the latter, he may be no better off in the end, and even be worse off".[5] Hence a better measure to know whether welfare of the agricultural sector has increased or decreased in the process of economic growth is to work out indices of the ratios of the prices received and prices paid by the farmers, commonly known as the parity indices. In other words, according to M.L. Singh, the precise measure of the relative change in the position of farmers as sellers and buyers is farmers' terms of trade.[6]

The purpose of parity index is to measure how far the prices of major agricultural commodities produced by the farmers kept pace with the prices of commodities purchased by them for consumption at home, or for the production of different crops. Given the basic data in regard to prices paid and prices received, a change in the base year can cause a substantial change not only in the magnitude but also in the direction of the terms of trade, particularly in situations where prices of one of the two sectors displayed large variations from year to year owing to low elasticity of demand and supply.

At present, all-India figures of farmers' terms of trade are not available. This is because of the differences of the products assuming different weights in the construction of the index number of prices received and prices paid in the various states; these figures are hardly comparable and so can hardly serve to indicate the all-India trends. Data regarding the ratio of prices received and paid by the farmers are available only for some states and those also for a limited period.

M.L. Singh presented data on farmers' terms of trade for twelve years, from 1951-52 to 1962-63, for five states, namely Assam, Kerala, Punjab, Orissa and West Bengal.[7] He found no systematic movement of the terms of trade in these states. In Punjab, the terms of trade for the farmers remained favourable for three years and unfavourable for the remaining nine years. The variations in the farmers' terms of trade are due to larger variations in the index of prices received than in the index of prices paid. Also, the non-farm items have a greater weightage in the index of the prices paid and the variation in the prices of these items have greatly influenced the prices paid index and the index of farmers' terms of trade. In Kerala, the terms of trade have changed against the farmers for all the ten years for which data are available. In Assam, on the other hand, the farmers' terms of trade remained, on the whole, favourable to the agriculturists except for three years. Similarly, in Orissa and West Bengal, no systematic movement of the terms of trade was observed. These differences in the behaviour of the terms of trade in different states arise partly because of different commodities with varying weightage represented in the computation of the terms of trade in different states, and partly because of the difference in the statistical representation of the terms of trade ratios.[8]

Further, M.L. Singh also observed that the trends of the farmers' terms of trade and the agricultural terms of trade were more or less similar in Punjab and Kerala only.

Table 3.1

Farmers' Terms of Trade and Agricultural Terms of Trade

Year	*Farmers Terms of Trade*				*Agricultural terms of trade*
	Assam	*Kerala*	*Orissa*	*Punjab*	
1952-53	100.0	100.0	100.0	100.0	100.0
1953-54	98.2	95.2	93.6	102.7	102.1
1954-55	95.9	85.2	103.4	91.3	94.2
1955-56	92.8	82.4	114.7	100.5	91.4
1956-57	102.7	83.4	123.2	105.2	98.6
1957-58	114.1	81.9	112.6	88.4	98.3
1958-59	105.2	83.0	110.7	104.7	101.8
1959-60	95.4	92.8		96.3	99.1
1960-61	103.4	92.1		96.4	98.4
1961-62	111.1	88.8		89.7	96.8
1962-63	101.6	84.1		86.2	93.5

Source: M.L.Singh, Sectoral Terms of Trade and Economic Growth in India (New Delhi, Sterling Publishers Pvt. Ltd., 1976), p. 53.

This is due to the fact that the farmers of these states greatly depend on non-farm products both for the purpose of consumption and production.

Since 'terms of trade' is an empirical concept, a large number of studies have been carried out to examine the movements in terms of trade in India.

The issue of domestic terms of trade in the Indian context was first of all discussed by N.K. Thingalaya by using the method of regression.[9] His conclusion was that up to the year 1940, terms of trade moved against agriculture and from then onwards moved in favour of it.

Some economists such as Nasir Ahmed Khan and K. Ohkawa

have advocated regulation of the terms of trade against the agricultural sector to mobilize the surplus of this sector to the urban sector.[10] If agricultural prices are depressed relative to non-agricultural prices, agricultural surplus will go into the hands of the non-agriculturists. Such a reduction in the terms of trade for agriculture will provide cheap food in the urban areas, reducing the wage in terms of industrial products. Profit wage ratio will be increased and more labourers could be provided with employment in the industrial sector. Khan argues the regulation of the terms of trade against agricultural sector on the assumption that the saving of this sector goes into unproductive channels. He believes that unfavourable agrticultural terms of trade will mobilize the savings of the agricultural sector to the industrial sector where they could be productively used.

The economists who believe in the mobilization of agricultural surplus through the regulation of terms of trade, however, do not see the unfavourable effects of negative price movements on the agricultural production. Khan believes that the marketed surplus of the agricultural sector is negatively correlated with the movement of agricultural terms of trade. A fall in the price is expected not to depress but to stimulate marketed surplus. It is argued that in the face of falling agricultural terms of trade, the farmers will be forced to curtail their consumption and sell more to get their fixed money requirements. On the other hand, rising agricultural terms of trade will lead them to consume more and sell less to get the same money income.[11]

Ashok Dhar examined the relative movements in the prices of agricultural commodities vis-a-vis the industrial goods for India for the period from 1952-53 to 1964-65.[12] He made use of the index number of wholesale prices constructed by the office of the Economic Adviser, Government of India. The weights used in the construction of composite index for the group of agricultural as well as industrial products were those adopted in the construction of the Economic Adviser's index number of wholesale prices. On the basis of his analysis, Dhar concluded that the terms of trade had moved in favour of the agricultural sector.

The first systematic estimates of agriculture's terms of trade in India were provided by R. Thamarajakshi for the period 1951-52 to 1965-66.[13] She calculated both net barter terms of trade and income terms of trade. The study revealed that during the period of the first three five-year plans, all prices received and paid by agriculturists, irrespective of the nature of the product used, showed an upward trend though at differential rates. In general, prices received by agriculture have risen at faster rate than those paid by agriculture and yet the consequent secular improvement (in favour of agriculture) in the net barter terms of trade is marginal. The income terms of trade have registered a significant rate of increase, thus indicating improved purchasing power of the agricultural sector for non-agricultural commodities.

M.L. Dantwala compared the relative price movements of agricultural commodities vis-a-vis industrial commodities for India during the period 1960-61 to 1973-74.[14] A comparison was made between the index number of wholesale prices of agricultural commodities and that of manufactures. The weight used for constructing the composite index for agriculture or the manufactured groups were those adopted in the construction of the Economic Adviser's index number of wholesale prices. He reached the conclusion that the terms of trade had moved in favour of agriculture.

M.L. Singh, in his study, revealed that the terms of trade between the agricultural and industrial sectors of the Indian economy showed a fluctuating trend, but, on the whole, remained unfavourable to the agricultural sector till 1962-63.[15] However, since the year 1964-65, they turned more sharply in favour of the agricultural sector. The sharp fluctuations in the terms of trade were largely prompted by a relatively great variability of agricultural prices.

Ashok Mitra measured domestic terms of trade between agriculture and industry from 1961-62 to 1973-74.[16] He mainly compared the price indices of three groups of commodities viz. agricultural products, foodgrains and manufactures. He observed that, in 1973-74, the official price index for food articles was

363.6, for foodgrains 400.71, for manufactures as a group 254.5, for machinery and equipment 244.5, and for finished products 238.6. His conclusions were based on the data obtained from the Reserve Bank of India Bulletins.

R. Thamarajakshi, in another study, examined the inter sectoral terms of trade for the period 1951-52 to 1973-74.[17] She prepared the annual composite price indices for all agricultural products sold by farmers and all non-agricultural products purchased by them. She used the Economic Adviser's index numbers of wholesale prices as price indicators in the case of both agricultural and industrial commodities. But for constructing the composite indices, she did not use the weights prepared by him. She found that, during the study period, while all prices received by agriculture rose by 5.94 per cent per annum, those paid by agriculture registered an increase of 4.45 per cent. Consequently, the net barter terms of trade improved in favour of agriculture at the rate of 1.43 per cent per annum.

L.R. Venkataraman, using the same methodology as adopted by Thamarajakshi, carried out the analysis for the period 1960-61 to 1973-74, and the results indicated that the terms of trade moved in favour of agriculture during this period.[18]

D.S. Tyagi has analysed the relative price position of agricultural commodities vis-a-vis manufactures during the past 50 years.[19] He pointed out that both in the pre-Independence and post-Independence period, movements in the terms of trade between agriculture and industry had been alternating.

According to his analysis, the following picture was obtained in the post-Independence period:—

(i) During the period from 1947-48 to 1952-53, terms of trade moved in favour of agriculture by about 5 per cent.

(ii) During the period from 1952-53 to 1961-62, terms of trade moved against agriculture. In six out of ten years, the terms of trade moved slightly in favour of industry.

(iii) During the period from 1961-62 to 1969-70, terms of trade moved in favour of agriculture in six out of nine years. On an average, agricultural prices were 20 per cent higher than industrial prices.

To sum up, the relative prices position of agricultural and industrial products has been changing from year to year. In some years prices of agricultural commodities increased at a comparatively fast rate while in other years, these lagged far behind the rise in prices of industrial products. On the whole, however, both appear to have moved upward.

Indradeep Sinha compared the index number of whole-sale prices of manufactured products and agricultural products for the period 1971-72 to 1976-77.[20] He has concluded that the terms of trade have turned against agriculture. Taking 100 per cent of commercial crops and 40 per cent of food crops as the marketed surplus of agriculture, his estimates of the loss suffered by agriculture on account of adverse terms of trade were Rs 900 crores in 1971-72, Rs 1,500 crores in 1975-76 and Rs 1,660 crores in 1976-77. The loss estimate for 1975-76 was also broadly confirmed by the Central Statistical Organisation (CSO) data according to which primary sector's factor income at 1970-71 prices declined from Rs 18,688 crores in 1974-75 to Rs.17,748 crores in 1975-76. This was primarily due to a fall in primary sector's price index from 172.2 in 1974-75 to 144.5 in 1975-76. When the weighted indices based on the CSO estimates of consumption expenditure were used, there was no material change in the results obtained, except that the net barter terms of trade now moved against agriculture from the year 1975-76 onwards instead of 1974-75.

A.S. Kahlon and D.S. Tyagi put to severe test some of the major ingredients of the methodology used by Thamarajakshi for estimating agriculture's barter as well as income terms of trade.[21] They not only criticized her method of quantifying agriculture's marketed surplus to domestic non-agriculture's which she used for estimating agriculture's income terms of trade but also questioned the validity of 'income terms of trade' as an analytical concept and, consequently, discarded it as misleading. They identified the pattern of trade between the two sectors with the help of National Sample Survey (NSS) consumption expenditure data for cultivator households (26th Round), the All-India Debt and Investment Survey and the National Accounts Statistics of the CSO. A commendable feature of the study was that the commodities purchased by the agricultural sector from non-agricultural sector included not only final consumption and intermediate consumption goods but also capital goods, the data for which had been lifted from the All-India Debt and Investment Survey. Again, instead of using a single year base, a three-year base period (i.e. 1969-70 to 1971-72) was used. Farm harvest prices, rather than wholesale price index number, were used as indicators of prices in the case of cereals, oil seeds, fibres, gur and tobacco. This was because the index numbers of wholesale prices had serious limitations in reflecting truly the prices received by the farmers for commodities sold to the non-agricultural sector. Using weighted indices based on NSS consumption expenditure data, the study found that, since 1974-75 terms of trade have moved against agriculture with the sharpest deterioration accruing in the sub-sector consisting of commodities sold for final consumption especially the field crops.

A substantial critique of Kahlon and Tyagi was provided by Nalini Vittal (1986, 1988).[22] Later D.S. Tyagi (1987)[23] reversed in some respects his earlier position of 1980.

R.Thamarajakshi made various attempts to examine inter-sectoral terms of trade (1963, 1969, 1977, 1985).[24] The author's latest study (1990) based on these earlier works examined the performance of agriculture in the Indian economy in the context of changing trends in the commodity terms of trade between agriculture and the rest of the economy.[25]

M.S. Rathore, A.L. Nadda and V.K. Singh have worked out wholesale prices and terms of trade of both the sectors in India during the period 1947-48 to 1977-78.[26] They have computed the relative prices and terms of trade on the basis of different base periods, and found out different turns of terms of trade. If earlier base periods such as 1952-53 = 100 and 1961-62 = 100 are taken, the terms of trade are favourable for the agricultural sector and if the base period of 1970-71 = 100 is taken the terms of trade are favourable for the industrial sector. They also examined the details of relative prices and terms of trade between 1947-48 and 1977-78 taking 1970-71 as the base. The terms of trade of food articles and manufactured articles showed that there had been only an increase of 6.75 points in 1977-78 above the index of 1947-48 in respect of food articles and the corresponding rise in respect of the manufactures articles had been of the order of 8.64 points in 1977-78 above that of 1947-48. It could be inferred that the agricultural sector had served as a reinforcing sector for the industrial sector.

Summing up, one finds that these studies have attempted to explain the sectoral interdependence in the form of terms of trade between agricultural commodities and industrial products. Relative prices of agricultural commodities and manufactured goods are useful signs of indicating the trends of resource flow between these two sectors via domestic terms of trade. Further, the degree of accuracy of the estimates of terms of trade depends upon a number of factors such as the reliability of weights used, the capacity of selected price/price indicators, the comprehensiveness of the identified pattern of trade, etc.

REFERENCES

1. (a) W.A.Lewis, "Economic Development with Unlimited Supplies of Labour", *The Manchester School of Economic and Social Studies,* (Vol. 22, May 1954), pp. 139-191.

   ————, "Unlimited Labour: Further Notes", *The Manchester School of Economic and Social Studies,* (Vol, 26, January, 1958).

   (b) R.S.Eckaus, "Factor Proportion Problem in Underdeveloped Areas", *American Economic Review* (Vol. 45, September, 1965), pp. 539-565.

   (c) N. Georgescu-Roegen. "Economic Theory and Agrarian Economics", *Oxford Economic Papers,* (12, February, 1960), pp.1-40.

(d) D.W. Jorgenson, "Development of a Dual Economy", *Economic Journal*, (Vol. 71, June, 1961), pp. 309-334.

(e) B.F. Johnston and J.W. Mellor, "The Role of Agriculture in Economic Development", *American Economic Review,* (Vol. 51, September, 1961), pp. 566-593.

(f) G. Ranis and J.C.H. Fei, "A Theory of Economic Development", *American Economic Review*, (Vol. 51, September, 1961), pp. 533-565.

2. Jacob Viner, *Studies in the Theory of International Trade*, (New York, Harper and Row, 1937), pp. 558-564.

3. (a) F.W. Taussig, *International Trade*, (New York, Macmillan, 1927).

(b) G.S. Dorrance, "The Income Terms of Trade", *Review of Economic Studies* (Vol. 16, No. 39, 1948-49), pp. 50-56.

(c) Jacob Viner, op.cit., pp. 558-564.

4. Jacob Viner, *Ibid.*

5. Government of India, Planning Commission, First Five-Year Plan, (1952), p.173.

6. M.L.Singh, *Sectoral Terms of Trade and Economic Growth of India*, (New Delhi, Sterling Publishers Pvt. Ltd., 1976), p.48.

7. M.L.Singh, op.cit., pp. 48-50.

8. N.K. Thingalaya, "Farmers' Terms of Trade in India", *Agricultural Situation in India,* (April, 1966), pp. 3-9.

9. N.K. Thingalaya, *Ibid.*

10. (a) N.A. Khan, "Resource Mobilization from Agriculture and Economic Development in India", *Economic Development and Cultural Change,* (Vol. 12, October, 1963), pp. 42-54.

(b) K. Ohkawa, "Balanced Growth and the Problem of Agriculture", *Historical Journal of Economics,* (Vol. 12, September, 1961), pp.13-15.

11. P.N. Mathur and H. Ezekiel, "Marketable Surplus of Food and Price Fluctuations in a Developing Economy", *Kyklos*, (Vol. 14, 1961), pp. 316-406.

12. Ashok Dhar, *Domestic Terms of Trade and Economic Development of India, 1952-53 to 1964-65.* (Ithaca, Cornell University, 1967).

13. R.Thamarajakshi, "Inter-Sectoral Terms of Trade and Marketed Surplus of Agricultural Produce, 1951-52 to 1965-66", *Economic and Political Weekly Review of Agriculture,* (Vol. IV, No. 26, June 28, 1968), pp. A-92 to A-102.

14. M.L. Dantwala, "Agricultural Policy since Independence", *Indian Journal of Agricultural Economics,* (vol. XXXI, No.4, October-December, 1976) pp. 31-53.

15. M.L.Singh, *op.cit.,*

16. Ashok Mitra, *Terms of Trade and Class Relations,* (New Jersey Frank Case and Co. 1977).

17. R.Thamarajakshi, "The Role of Price Incentives in Stimulating Agricultural Production in a Developing Economy", in Dougles Ensminger (ed.) *Food Enough or Starvation for Millions,* (New Delhi, Tata McGraw Hill, 1977), pp. 376-390.

18. L.R. Venkataraman, "Foodgrains Growth and Price Policy", in C.H. Shahed, *Agricultural Development of India, Policy and Problems*, (New Delhi, Orient Longman Ltd., 1979), pp.199-235.

19. D.S. Tyagi, "Farm Prices and Class Bias in India", *Economic and Political Weekly,* (Vol. 24, No. 39, September 29, 1979), pp. A-111 to A-124.

20. Indradeep Sinha, *The Changing Agrarian Scene: Problems Tasks,* (New Delhi, People's Publishing House, 1980).

21. A.S. Kahlon, and D.S. Tyagi, "Inter-Sectoral Terms of Trade", *Economic and Political Weekly*, (vol. XV, No.52, December 27, 1980), pp. A-173 to A-184.

22. Nalini Vittal, "Intersectoral Terms of Trade in India: A Study of Concept and Method", *Economic and Political Weekly,* (December 27, 1986), p. A-147.

__________, "Intersectoral Terms of Trade in India: Reality and Hype", *Economic and Political Weekly*, (September 24, 1988).

23. D.S. Tyagi, "Intersectoral Terms of Trade: Misconceptions and Fairy Tales", *Economic and Political Weekly,* (vol. XXIII, No.17, April 23, 1988), pp.858-864.

24. R.Thamarajakshi, Intersectoral Terms of Trade Revisited", *Economic and Political Weekly,* (Vol. XXV, No.13, March 31, 1990), pp. A-48 to A-52.

25. R.Thamarajakshi, *Ibid.*, pp. A-48 to A-51.

26. M.S. Rathore, A.L. Nadda and V.K. Singh, "Inter-Sectoral Terms of Trade in India, 1947-1978", *Indian Journal of Agricultural Economics,* (Vol. 34, No.4, Conference Number, October-December, 1979), pp. 66 to 75.

4

Marketed Surplus and Marketable Surplus

FOR the rapid economic growth of an under-developed country like India, an increase in agricultural production is indispensable. But to sustain the tempo of development, an overall increase in agricultural production or agricultural productivity in general may not be sufficient in itself. From the point of view of growth and development of an economy, an increase in agricultural production loses much of its significance unless it is followed by an increase in marketable and marketed suplus of agricultural products.

The importance of marketable surplus has been generally viewed from three angles viz. food surplus, industrialisation and economic growth. In a developing country, marketable surplus of agricultural products has an extremely significant role to play. The rate at which agricultural production expands, affording an increasing supply of food and raw materials, largely determines the pace of economic development. W.H. Nicholls highlights the significance of rising marketed surplus and asserts, "Until under-developed countries succeed in achieving and sustaining (either through domestic production or imports) a reliable food surplus, they have not fulfilled the fundamental preconditions for economic development".[1]

Thus, by raising output and marketed surplus of foodgrains, farmers can make positive contribution to economic development. Therefore, peasants have to be induced not only to provide more but also to part with a larger surplus to feed non-farm population.

As development proceeds and non-agricultural occupations and non-rural centres of population grow in importance, the importance, as also the difficulty, of mobilising marketed surplus grows. In the case of developing countries, the problem is further complicated by the overall inadequacies of the country's productive capacity in agriculture, both absolutely and relatively to needs.

In India, the farmers produce foodgrains and cash crops like cotton, jute, oil seeds and sugarcane. Cash crops are available mostly for the market; the retentions by the farmers, being only a small proportion of total production, do not present serious problems of mobilisation. The real problem of mobilisation arises with regard to foodgrains because farmers are both producers as well as consumers of foodgrains. They dispose of only what is in excess of their requirements. Thus the flow of marketed surplus of foodgrains can be a major limiting factor in the process of industrialization.

In this connection, M.Dobb writes, "There is a reason to suppose that it will be the marketed surplus of agriculture which plays the crucial role in the under-developed country in setting the limits to the possible rate of industrialization".[2]

In brief, in the case of an under-developed country, the marketed surplus in the agricultural sector is of crucial significance from the following points of view:—

(i) An increase in the marketed surplus helps in releasing some labour force from agricultural to non-agricultural sector. When marketed surplus increases, some workers can be shifted from agricultural to industrial sector, causing no decline in the agricultural output. The underlying idea has been depicted in the models prepared by W.A.Lewis, and G. Ranis and John C.H. Fei (1961).[3] In their original model, they were mainly concerned with the inter-sectoral flow of labour and marketable surplus from agriculture.

In whatever manner a particular growth model is

framed, the underlying idea remains that agricultural sector must become an object of manipulation for extracting and appropriating surpluses (in the form of reproductible capital, labour force, etc.) for economic development.

(ii) It would initiate the programme of rapid industrialization as the export of marketed surplus helps in importing capital goods and other necessary raw materials.

(iii) Marketable surplus from the agricultural sector would contribute to capital formation in the non-agricultural sector. Rise in the income of the farmers stimulates the demand for industrial products and raises the profits of the capitalists and thus their savings.

(iv) It would contribute to an improvement in the standard of living in the agricultural sector by making available to it the industrial consumer goods.

(v) It also generates the demand for industrial products and leads to the existence of market.

Thus, we find that in order to sustain an increasing tempo of development, it is important that the magnitude as well as the flow of marketable surplus should be augmented.

The crucial role of mobilising agricultural surpluses in economic development is illustrated by the experience of countries such as Soviet Russia, Japan, China and Poland. In Russia, increase in the flow of marketable surplus was achieved by collective farming and by the setting up of large-scale state farms which acted as agencies for channelling a larger percentage of the surplus to the urban sector. The system of compulsory delivery contracts at fixed prices not only provided the non-agricultural sector with a guaranteed supply of agricultural produce but also enabled the farmers to maximise their produce.

China organised agrarian cooperatives which resulted in substantial increase in agricultural production and made possible the transfer of a large part of it to the state government at fixed rate.

In Japan, the increased use of fertilizers and adoption of improved techniques led to considerable expansion of domestic output which outstripped population growth. But a large part of the agricultural surplus was siphoned off by the government for capital formation, through heavy land taxes. Land taxation played in Japan the same role as compulsory grain collections from collective farms played in Soviet Russia.

In Poland, the increase in the flow of marketable surplus has been brought about by the offer of various incentives to peasants like greater credit facilities, increased supply of consumer goods and even by reversing its investment policy. Compulsory grain levies have also been adopted in Poland.

Theoretically, a distinction is generally made between marketed surplus and marketable surplus.

a) Marketed Surplus or Objective Approach

In objective approach, marketed surplus (or market arrivals) refers to the amount actually brought into the market for sale. It is usually meant for the non-farm rural as well as urban population. Marketed surplus does not depend on production alone but also on farmer's behaviour regarding retention on farm.

b) Marketable Surplus or Subjective Approach

In subjective approach, marketable surplus represents the theoretical surplus available for disposal with the producer, left after his genuine requirements of family consumption, payment of wages in kind, feed, seed and wastage have been met.

Thus while marketable surplus refers to the potential surplus available for disposal with the producer, marketed surplus represents only that portion of the marketable surplus which is actually sold.

'Marketed surplus' may be less than, equal to or even more than 'marketable surplus' depending upon the external factors operating in the market economy. The 'marketable surplus' and 'marketed surplus' will be equal only under ideal conditions.

Divergence between the two arises on account of the fact that what is marketable need not all be marketed in a given period but added to stocks on account of the following factors:

(i) Poor farmers may sell out of distress and repurchase later, usually at higher prices. For such farmers, marketable surplus may very well be negative. Or, in other words, marketed surplus may very well be more than the marketable surplus.

(ii) Rich farmers, on the other hand, may prefer to keep whole or part of their surplus in stocks. For such farmers, marketable surplus could be larger than the marketed surplus.

(iii) The carry-over stocks from the previous period may be marketed in a particular period.

According to P.N. Mathur and H. Ezekiel, use of the term 'marketable surplus' depends upon the character of an economy.[4] In developed countries, producers of foodgrains retain whatever is necessary for their own consumption and sell the surplus in the market. On the other hand, in a developing economy, farmers sell that amount of output which will provide them the necessary cash and retain the balance of their output for self-consumption.

M.V. Nadkarni distinguishes between gross marketed surplus and net marketed surplus.[5] Gross marketed surplus refers to the actually marketed quantities and net marketed surplus is the gross marketed surplus minus repurchase of foodgrains.

Similarly, net marketable surplus refers to marketable surplus net of the purchase of foodgrains of all producers, while gross marketable surplus is the sum of positive marketable surplus of all rural households.

A large number of studies have been conducted in this field. Broadly, we can classify these studies into three categories:

(1) The first set of studies showing relationship between marketable surplus and economic development.

(2) The second set of studies showing responsiveness of marketable surplus to price and output.

(3) The third set of studies showing the responsiveness of marketable surplus to size of holdings.

Relationship between Marketable Surplus and Economic Development

The studies showing the relationship between marketable surplus and economic development can be further grouped under two sub-categories. The studies under first sub-category show how marketable surplus is a crucial constraint on industrialisation. They stress the role of marketable surplus from agriculture mainly from the point of view of the urban sector which must have adequate supply of wage goods to support its labour at as low a cost as possible. W.H. Nicholls emphasized that agriculture must first be developed enough to generate sizeable marketable surplus before any measures towards industrialisation were contemplated.[6] The second sub-category of studies, most of which adopt Marxian analytical framework, deals with the process of generation of marketable surplus.

Responsiveness of Marketable Surplus to Price and Output

P.N. Mathur—Ezekiel study showed an inverse relationship between price and marketed surplus based on the assumption of fixed cash requirement.[7] They proposed that small and medium farmers in a developing country sold only that much amount of output which would provide them the money necessary to satisfy their cash requirements. This tended to make short-run supply curve of foodgrains backward bending. Thus, the residual was the amount of output which was retained for consumption and not the amount of output which was sold.

V.M. Dandekar, however, pointed out that Mathur—Ezekiel proposition was valid only for a small and very special class of farmers, who had very little of other sources of cash income.[8] He argued that for a large class of small farmers, their own production was not sufficient to meet their needs. They sold little of it and derived their cash income from other sources to meet their needs for cash. Therefore, according to him, if the prices of foodgrains affected the farmers at all, they affected them more as consumers and less as producers.

T.N. Krishnan showed that the inverse relationship between price and marketed surplus postulated by Mathur—Ezekiel could be derived independently of any assumption about the fixity of farmers' requirements for cash.[9]

The study conducted by P.N. Mathur and S. Prakash showed that the extent of marketed surplus was affected by cash requirements.[10]

These studies have, in general, dealt with responsiveness to both prices and output.

Responsiveness of Marketable Surplus to Size of Holdings

A large number of studies have been conducted, both at national and inter-state levels, to examine the responsiveness of marketable surplus to size of holdings. Dharam Narain studies the reponsiveness of marketable surplus to size of holdings for the year 1950-51.[11] The study was based on indirect estimation at the national level. He used mainly National Sample Survey (NSS) data on land holdings and consumer expenditure. Marketable surplus was defined as the difference between all agricultural output and retentions. He found that marketable surplus as a proportion of output declined as the size of holdings increased up to 10-15 acres. It increased steadily thereafter. His results showed that small farmers' contribution to marketable surplus was sizeable. He found the shape of supply curve to be backward bending.

Utsa Patnaik conducted a study on the distribution of marketable surplus by size-group of holdings.[12] Her study was based on indirect estimation, covering aggregative data at the national level for 1960-61. She found that farms up to 10 acres contributed 33.2 per cent and those up to 15 acres 44.4 per cent of total marketable surplus of all farms.

P.S. Sharma conducted another study for the year 1960-61 (based on indirect estimation) both at the national and the state level.[13] It was found that size-class up to 5 acres was having a negative marketable surplus at the national level and also in almost all the states (except a few). The size-class of 5 to 10 acres was observed to be deficit in two states, and for other states and at the national level, it showed a positive surplus. The proportion of marketable surplus to net production of foodgrains also increased consistently with increase in the size of holdings.

The size of the farm as a determining factor for the marketable surplus was revealed by the data based on the studies in Economic of Farm Management in Punjab.[14] The data regarding distribution of important agricultural commodities marketed per holding during three years (1967-68, 1968-69 and 1969-70) confirmed the fact that for four commodities viz. wheat, gram, maize and paddy, the marketed surplus per holding increased with the increase in the size of holdings. Further, barring a few exceptions, marketable surplus as a percentage of production plus opening balance, increased with increase in the size of holdings. In other words, the small size of holdings was a serious limiting factor in increasing the size of marketable surplus.

Another study at district level in Punjab was conducted and the results were presented in the Bench Mark Survey for 1970-71.[15] The study supported the argument that in the case of wheat and maize, there was a considerable difference in the disposal of surplus produce of big (79.87 per cent), small (70 per cent) and marginal farmers (38-81 per cent). All these categories of farmers disposed of their produce after making provision for domestic consumption and seed requirements. No tendency for holding back the produce for sale in off-season was observed.

S.S. Johl in his study on the 'Gains of Green Revolution' admitted that the gains to the farmers were directly proportional to the marketed surplus that each one of them could generate.[16] The big farmers were found to have larger marketed surplus in total quantities as well as per hectare.

Darbara Singh and K.S. Gill examined in their study the level of marketable surplus and the marketing pattern of important crops adopted by the Punjab farmers.[17] The production, consumption and marketable surplus for the selected crops are reproducted in Table 4.1. It showed that for foodgrains, the larger holdings possessed the highest marketable surplus and smaller holdings the lowest. Singh and Gill also computed per unit production, consumption and marketable surplus for wheat (reproduced in Table 4.2). The yield (per acre) obtained by smaller category (1) was the highest but man-land ratio being low at the small and marginal holdings, they could spare lesser marketable surplus per unit.

Table 4.1

Consumption Pattern with the Selected Holdings (consumption as percentage to total production, 1978-79)

Category	*Family consumption*	*Seed*	*Concentrates*	*Payment to laboures*	*Artisans*	*Others*	*Total*	*Marketabls surplus*
				Wheat				
1.	18.08	2.58	3.46	1.73	2.25	1.73	29.83	70.17
2.	15.84	2.24	2.45	1.63	1.53	2.86	26.55	73.45
3.	10.59	2.40	1.92	1.09	1.16	1.65	18.79	82.21
4.	9.44	2.57	1.80	1.94	0.98	0.86	17.59	82.41
				Paddy				
1.							2.91	97.09
2.							2.92	97.08
3.							4.32	95.69
4.							2.66	97.34

				Maize				
1.	37.50	2.50	-	-	7.50	8.33	55.83	44.17
2.	32.80	3.22	-	0.46	6.37	7.59	50.44	49.56
3.	19.89	1.68	-	3.68	3.81	3.91	32.97	67.03
4.	13.74	1.77	-	3.98	2.71	2.32	24.52	75.48
				Groundnut*				
1.	-						-	-
2.	15.22						15.22	84.78
3.	14.89						14.89	85.11
4.	16.78						16.78	83.22
				Cotton*				
1.	31.38						31.58	88.42
2.	19.53						19.53	80.47
3.	16.90						16.90	83.10
4.	16.78						16.78	83.22

***Note:** (a) In case of groundnut and cotton, family consumption includes seeds also.

(b) Category — Operational Size of holdings

1. 0 to 7 acres — 6.00
2. 7.1 to 12 acres — 9.62
3. 12.1 to 20 acres — 16.90
4. 20.1 and above — 25.27

Source: Darbara Singh and K.S. Gill, "Marketable Surplus and Pattern of Marketing of Important Crops Followed in Punjab State: A case study", *Agricultural Marketing*, (Ludhiana, Department of Economic and Sociology, PAU, July, 1981.)

K.S. Dhindsa and Jaspal Singh examined time pattern of marketed surplus of foodgrains by farm-size for Punjab.[18] The relationship between production, retention and marketed surplus of wheat and paddy on the sample farms is shown in Table 4.3. Out of total production of 863 quintals of wheat with small farmers, they retained 534 quintals of wheat i.e. 61.88 per cent, and marketed the balance produce of 329 quintals i.e. 38.12 per cent. In respect of medium and large farmers, the study showed that the percentage shares of retention and marketed surplus were

54.89 and 45.11, and 40.85 and 59.15 per cent, respectively. In respect of paddy, the empirical results showed that at small, medium and large farm levels, the farmers retained 19.01, 20.08, 17.02 per cent of productions, respectively and the marketed surpluses were as high as 80.99, 79.92 and 82.98 per cent, respectively. It was thus apparent that small and medium farmers held a large percentage of their production of foodgrains for family needs and other payment, compared to the big farmers. The study also showed that a large percentage of wheat production was retained at the farm level, compared to the corresponding figures for paddy. The major items of retention, as revealed by the study, were food for family consumption, feeds, seeds and payment of labour in kind.

Table 4.2

Per acre Marketable Surplus for Wheat with the Selected Holdings

Category	*Area under wheat (acres)*	*Yield qtls/ per acre*	*Production (qtls)*	*Consumption at the farm (qtls)*	*Total marketable surplus (qtls)*	*Per acre marketable surplus (qtls)*
1.	4.18	13.84	57.82	17.24	40.58	9.71
2.	7.30	13.35	98.05	26.05	72.00	10.54
3.	12.60	13.67	172.25	30.70	141.55	11.24
4.	19.67	13.67	268.75	44.58	224.17	11.40

Source: Darbara Singh and K.S. Gill, *op. cit.*

Table 4.3

Production, marketed surplus and retention of wheat and paddy by farm size (1978-79)

Farm size	*Production*	*Retention*	*Marketed Surplus*
		Wheat	
Small	863 (100.0)	534 (61.88)	329 (38.12)
Medium	4201 (100.0)	2306 (54.89)	1895 (45.1)

Large	4935	2016	2919
	(100.0)	(40.85)	(59.15)
Overall	9999	4856	5143
	(100.0)	(48.56)	(51.45)
		Paddy	
Small	1642	312	1330
	(100.0)	(19.00)	(80.99)
Medium	8780	1763	7017
	(100.0)	(20.08)	(79.92)
Large	10974	1868	9106
	(100.0)	(17.02)	(82.98)
Overall	21396	3943	17453
	(100.0)	(18.43)	(81.57)

Note 1. Figures in brackets are percentages to total production.

Source: K.S. Dhindsa and Jaspal Singh, *op.cit.*

From these studies, one can conclude that mobilisation of marketed/marketable surplus plays a crucial role not only in the economic development of the country but also in the context of the relationship between the agricultural and non-agricultural sectors of a country. The extent of the marketable surplus of a commodity depends very largely on the consumption requirements of the people, within a producing area, the nature of the crop, relative price levels of different farm products, the economic status of the farm population, size of holdings, taxation and government policy.

REFERENCES

1. W.H. Nicholls, "The Place of Agriculture in Economic Development", in Eicher and Witt(ed.), *Agriculture in Economic Development,* (New York, McGraw Hill, 1962), p.1.
2. M.Dobb, *On Economic Theory and Socialism : Collected Papers,* (London and Boston, Routledge and Kegan Paul Ltd., 1955).
3. (a) W.A.Lewis, "Economic Development with Unlimited Supplies

of Labour", *The Manchester School of Economic and Social Studies* (Vol. 22, May, 1954), pp.131-191.

(b) Gustav Ranis and John C.H.Fei, "A Theory of Economic Development", *Asian Economic Review,* (vol. 51, No.4, September, 1961), pp.535-565.

4. P.N. Mathur and H.Ezekiel, "Marketable Surplus of Food and Price Fluctuations in a Developing Economy", *Kyklos,* (vol. 14, 1961), pp.396-408.

5. 'M.V. Nadkarni, *Marketable Surplus and Market Dependence in a Millet Region,* (New Delhi, Allied Publishers Pvt. Ltd., 1986).

6. (a) C.N. Vakil and P.R. Brahmananda, *Planning for an Expanding Economy*, (Bombay, Vora and Company, Publishers (P) Ltd., 1956).

   (b) William H. Nicholls, "An Agricultural Surplus as a Factor in Economic Development", *Journal of Political Economy,* (vol.71, No.1, February, 1963), pp.1-29.

   (c) William H. Nicholls, "The Place of Agriculture in Economic Development", in Eicher and Witt (ed.) *Agriculture in Economic Development,* (New York, McGraw Hill, 1962), pp.11-44.

7. P.N. Mathur and H.Ezekiel, *op.cit.*, pp.396-408.

8. V.M. Dandekar, "Prices, Production and Marketed Surplus of Foodgrains", *Indian Journal of Agricultural Economics,* (vol. 19, Nos. 3 and 4, July-Dec. 1964), pp. 186-195.

9. T.N. Krishnan, "The Marketable Surplus of Foodgrains", *Economic and Political Weekly,* (vol. 17, Annual Number, Feb,. 1965).

10. P.N. Mathur, and S. Prakash, "Inventory Behaviour of Indian Agriculture and Its Effect on General Price Level", *First Conference on Inventory Management*, (Budapest, 1980).

11. Dharm Narain, *Distribution of Marketed Surplus of Agricultural Produce by Size-Level of Holdings in India*: *1950-51* (Asia, 1961).

12. Utsa Patnaik, "Contribution to the Output and Marketable Surplus of Agricultural Products by Cultivating Groups in India, 1960-61", *Economic and Political Weekly*, (vol. X, No.52, December 27, 1975), pp.A-90 to A-100.

13. Prem S.Sharma, "Estimation of Marketable Surplus of Foodgrains by Size-Classes of Holdings in Rural Cultivating Households - A

Physical Approach", *Agricultural Situation in India,* (vol. 27, No.5, August, 1972), pp. 327-335.

14. The Economic Adviser to Government, Punjab, *Economics of Agricultural Production and Farm Management in Punjab: 1967-68, 1968-69 and 1969-70*, Economic and Statistical Organisation, Punjab, Chandigarh.
15. Ranjit Singh, *Report on Bench Mark Survey, Small Farmers Development Agency (Sangrur and Patiala Districts),* (Department of Agriculture Punjab, Chandigarh, May 10, 1973).
16. S.S. Johl, "Gains of the Green Revolution: "How They Have Been Shared in Punjab", *Journal of Development Studies*, (vol. 11, No.3, April, 1975), pp. 178-189.
17. Darbara Singh and K.S. Gill, "Marketable Surplus and Pattern of Marketing of Important Crops Followed in Punjab State: A Case Study", *Agricultural Marketing,* (Department of Economics and Sociology, PAU, Ludhiana, July, 1981).
18. K.S. Dhindsa and Jaspal Singh, "Marketed Surplus of Wheat and Paddy by Farm Size in Punjab - A Case Study", *Margin* (vol.15, No.2, January, 1983), pp. 81-82.

5

Taxation and Expenditure Benefits

Taxation: An Instrument of Surplus Mobilisation

The chief aim of a developing country is economic development. Development necessitates mobilisation of surpluses. Taxation is considered to be one of the important instruments of surplus mobilisation.

Fiscal economists, too, have emphasized resource mobilisation for development purposes in an economy like India's as being the primary task of fiscal policy. In the words of Raja J. Chelliah, "The fundamental principle underlying the tax structure (of a developing economy like that of India) should be the principle of mobilisation of economic surplus—and (channelling) it into investment without, in the process, destroying or gravely restricting its occurrence".[1] An efficient and effective tax system is the basic requirement of fiscal reform in a developing economy.

The very process of development helps create 'economic surpluses' in many areas of an under-developed country like India. Not only this, there are certain classes of people who benefit more from this process than others. Hence there is a need to mop up this surplus from the point of view of equity also.

A major part of the national income in an under-developed country originates in the agricultural sector, and therefore, it would be reasonable to expect that sector to provide a major part of resources for development. This sector has to be taxed not only because it has a potential surplus, but also in order to increase the surplus.

A large number of tax incidence studies were conducted in India both at the state level and at the national level. These studies attempted to measure tax incidence via consumption approach. In particular, these studies were concerned with equity in taxation between the agricultural and the non-agricultural sector and with the determination of relative tax incidence among the different income-expenditure groups in the two sectors. A brief review of these studies will help us to place the various conclusions derived from these studies in proper perspective.

The first tax incidence study in India, was conducted by the Taxation Enquiry Committee in 1924-25[2]. The Committee was asked to determine what the weight of taxation was on particular social classes which, in this context, meant occupational groups. But these occupational groups were very heterogeneous and could not readily be related to their ability to pay.

The Taxation Enquiry Commission, 1953-54, making the first systematic study of tax incidence in this country, brought out the relative under-taxation of the rural sector.[3] The Commission attributed the lower incidence of indirect taxes in the rural sector to the insufficient monetization of rural consumption. But in the absence of any classification of population by income levels, the study was restricted to indirect taxes and it related tax payment to consumer expenditure (cash and non-cash) as indicated by the National Sample Survey (NSS), 14th Round. It confined itself to the concept of horizontal equity. The study showed that, in 1953-54, the tax incidence i.e. direct money burden of Union and state indirect taxes, absolutely as well as relatively, was very much low in the rural sector as compared to the urban sector. It further showed that the inter-sectoral difference in favour of the rural sector was the greatest in the top household expenditure class (Rs. 300 and above per month). Per capita tax payment by rural households in that expenditure class was two-fifths lower than that by urban households in the same group. Over the subsequent five years i.e. up to 1958-59, the incidence of Union and State indirect taxes on either sector increased substantially. But the relative burden of indirect taxes on the rural sector diminished somewhat. This was revealed in a study made by the Ministry of Finance.[4] This study was similar in methodology and coverage to that of the Taxation Enquiry Commission (1953-54).

Another study of the Government of India, benefiting from the detailed expenditure tabulations provided by the 18th Round (1963-64) of the NSS, worked out new estimates of tax content in the expenditure of both rural and urban households.[5] The study assumed full shiftability of indirect taxes. For measuring the tax incidence, consumption approach was followed. But the study cautioned that this measure tended to overstate the progression or understate regression of the tax system since the consumer expenditure as a proportion of income tends to fall as one moves up the income scale. Though the study employed the estimates of per capita consumer expenditure as yielded by the NSS data, some adjustments were made to make them consistent with the official estimates of National Income for 1963-64. The study clarified that the money burden of indirect taxes was more on the urban than on the rural sector. Progression was more in the former than in the latter sector. This applied not only to all the households taken together but also to households at different expenditure levels.

K.N. Raj, extended the study of tax incidence to direct taxes.[6] He allocated both direct and indirect taxes collected by the Union and State Governments in 1952-53 to 1957-58 to the rural and urban sectors on the basis of a rough approximation. However, his analysis showed that:

(1) during the period 1952-53 to 1957-58, tax as percentage of income in the rural sector was about one-third of that in the urban sector;

(2) the increase in tax revenue since 1952-53 had been realised more from the urban than the rural sector; and

(3) while government taxation had probably adsorbed nearly 40 per cent of the increase in income in the urban sector, the share of the government in the increased income of the rural sector had been perhaps not more than 15 per cent.

E.T. Mathew studied the problem of tax incidence in India on the basis of the net tax burden or fiscal burden.[7] Mathew calculated the burden of taxation in the sense of formal incidence. He allocated the total Central and State tax revenue between the agricultural and non-agricultural sectors in 1958-59 and found that the former paid 6.8 per cent and the latter 9.2 per cent of its income in taxes. Mathew worked out the 'net burden' though he took into consideration only relevant social and development expenditures on revenue account, such as agricultural and rural development, irrigation, multipurpose river valley schemes, veterinary service, community projects, national extension service, local development works, education, and medical and public health service. Based on relevant assumptions, he then allocated the benefits from these services between agricultural and non-agricultural sectors and arrived at the net tax/income ratios of 3.2 per cent and 7.3 per cent, respectively. He also concluded that the tax burdens were progressively distributed in the non-agricultural sector but not in the agricultural sector. Mathew, however, did not allocate the benefits of investment expenditure nor did he consider the indirect effects which might spill over from one sector to another.

A more comprehensive and systematic study was made by Ved P. Gandhi.[8] His study covered all the direct and indirect taxes levied both by the Central Government and the State Government. Gandhi worked out the relative tax burden on the agricultural and non-agricultural sectors during the years 1950-51 to 1961-62. For calculating the relative taxable capacity of the two sectors, Gandhi assumed the 30th percentile of the population in the two sectors as having no taxable capacity and having only subsistence or below subsistence income. On comparing his estimates of relative taxable capacity and relative tax payments in the agricultural and non-agricultural sectors, Gandhi concluded that there was a clear indication of inter-sectoral inequity in favour of the agricultural sector. The exact extent of inequity was difficult to state. Gandhi also worked out the incidence of public expenditure on both agricultural and non-agricultural sectors. He considered expenditure on revenue account only and concluded that the benefits received by the agricultural sector were more than the taxes paid by this sector.

He also made a study of the inter-class inequity in the distribution of tax (both direct and indirect) burden as between agricultural and non-agricultural sectors. His findings highlight that both lower and upper income groups of agricultural sector have borne a significantly lesser average tax burden and marginal tax burden during the years 1950-51 to 1960-61 than have their counterparts in the non-agricultural sector.

Ved P. Gandhi made another attempt to measure the tax burden on Indian agriculture.[9] He observed that the sectoral tax burden defined as the ratio of taxes per capita to income per capita of the sector had various shortcomings. For example, it assumed proportionality of taxes. It also assumed that if income alone was the indicator of taxable capacity, the wealth per capita, the degree of wealth inequality and income inequality were not given due consideration. The expenditure side of the budget, too, would be neglected. On all these accounts, he found that the agricultural sector was under-taxed. Gandhi's study also took cognizance of open and concealed taxes and open and concealed subsidies.

H.F. Lydall and M. Ahmed conducted a study for the year 1965-66.[10] The merit of the study was that the incidence of almost all the direct and indirect taxes was calculated according to income groups in the rural and urban sectors for the first time in India. The basic exercise was done for the year 1965-66. Estimates for 1965-66 were made on certain assumptions about the rates of growth of relevant variables involved, assuming the same income distribution. Income distribution for India as a whole (later on, the all-India figures were broken into rural and urban distribution) was ascertained with the help of income tax statistics and NSS data on consumer expenditure. Direct taxes were allocated directly to the relevant income groups and indirect taxes to various income groups on the basis of the estimated pattern of consumption. Consumption pattern was estimated with the use of Engel curve.

S.L. Shetty presented the estimates and analysis of relative taxable capacity and tax burden in respect of farm and non-farm sectors in India during the first eighteen years of planning.[11] These estimates and analyses, undertaken at the aggregative sectoral level, formed the first part of a comprehensive examination of the hypothesis that the farm sector in India was under-taxed. The other part compared (i) inter-class analysis of tax burden in the two sectors and (ii) the estimates of potential tax revenue which the farm sector would have given to the state exchequer if, based on inter-sectoral equity, it was also subjected to the identical incidence levels as those borne by the non-farm sector. He worked out both absolute taxable capacity and relative taxable capacity. Considering the difference in the taxable capacity of the two sectors, he asserted that if progressivity was desired to the extent of 1.9, the relative tax burden between the two sectors would become equitably distributed. Further, he concluded that the tax burdens on farm and non-farm sectors had significantly increased during the Second and Third Plan periods. He also computed the elasticity co-efficients of tax burdens with respect to sectoral income by fitting the regression line.

$$y = a\,x^b$$

where y = tax yield, b = elasticity co-efficient,

x = sectoral income.

Shetty also measured the inter-class burden of taxation by juxtaposing two sets of data: the data on income distribution and the data on tax burdens at different income levels.[12] He concluded that among the three income groups, the low and middle income groups in the non-farm sector did not appear to have significantly higher incidence than the incidence on the corresponding groups in the farm sector, whereas the top income bracket in the non-farm experienced a far higher incidence of taxation than the corresponding class in the farm sector.

K.S.R.N. Sarma and M.J.K. Thavaraj have critically examined different studies on the tax incidence in India and discovered several conceptual and empirical shortcomings therein.[13] First of all, definitions of the basic concepts of 'incidence' and 'equity' were examined. Further, the problem of the concept of net fiscal burden was analysed. Ved P. Gandhi and E.T. Mathew, had attempted to study the problem of incidence on the basis of 'net benefit'.[14] Both these studies took into consideration only public expenditure under revenue account. Capital expenditure was excluded on the ground that the benefits generated by the capital projects were usually spread over a long period so that it was too difficult to work out the annual value of benefits. While Gandhi had taken into consideration all public expenditure on revenue account, Mathew had confined exclusively to development expenditure.

K.N. Reddy estimated the inter-sectoral fiscal burden by covering the tax burden borne by a sector on the one hand, and the benefits received from public expenditure on the other.[15] In addition to Central and State taxes, he took into consideration taxes levied by local authorities. On the side of taxation, he, too, used the term incidence in the formal sense. He also paid some attention to the concealed taxes (i.e. additional costs which the agricultural sector has to bear for education and health services) as well as concealed subsidies (lower irrigation and electricity rates, cheap finance provided to the agricultural sector, etc.). He mainly concluded that there was no inequity in the burden between the agricultural and non-agricultural sector and between the lower income classes of the two sectors. However, there was inequity between the upper income classes of the two sectors in favour of the agriculture sector.

The Economic Times Research Bureau examined the inequality in tax incidence both at the inter-sector and inter-class levels in India.[16] The Bureau assumed that the incidence of income tax, corporation tax, expenditure tax, estate duty, wealth tax, gift tax, profession tax, urban immovable property tax, entertainment duty and electricity duty fell entirely on the non-agricultural sector. Only the incidence of land revenue fell 100 per cent on the agricultural sector. Other taxes were apportioned on the basis of certain plausible assumptions. The Bureau observed that the agricultural sector was substantially under-taxed. In the agricultural sector, households with cultivated land of 10 acres and above paid only Rs.14 crores towards agricultural income tax while households with an annual income of Rs. 3,500 and above in the non-agricultural sector paid direct taxes to the tune of Rs. 917 crores in 1969-70.

One more attempt made in this direction was that of Indirect Taxation Enquiry Committee (1977) which measured the incidence of indirect taxes for 1973-74.[17] Basically, the methodology employed in the study was the same as that used in the earlier three works, but with some improvement in respect of measurement of input taxation, allocation of sales tax burden and apportionment of the tax borne by the government. Similarly, attempts were made to allocate the burden of electricity duty on the basis of its purpose-wise collections. No attempt was made to measure the burden of direct taxation.

A most comprehensive and methodologically sound study of incidence of indirect taxes was carried out by Raja J. Chelliah and Ram N. Lal for 1973-74.[18] This study covered all Central and State indirect taxes (excluding export duties) and presented estimates of distribution of (i) aggregate burden of indirect taxes (ii) incidence of Central and State indirect taxes separately, and (iii) incidence by types of goods. The study indicated a progressive pattern of indirect taxation.

T. Divakara Rao's study made a modest attempt to measure the changes in the tax burden in India for the years 1964-65, 1968-69 and 1975-76.[19] The study also covered the allocation of tax burden of direct and indirect taxes among various income classes. But it did not take into account the benefits of public expenditure.

S.S. Johl's analysis suggested that the agricultural sector in India was taxed lightly as compared to the non-agricultural sector of the economy.[20] He also observed that this tax burden was decreasing over period of time and the additional incomes were taxed very nominally.

The above mentioned studies estimated and analysed the incidence of taxation between agricultural and non-agricultural sectors. However, there are some studies which were confined to the agricultural sector only. A brief review of such studies follows.

N.A. Khan maintained that the most important sector in which investible surpluses could be generated was agriculture.[21] He further argued that though the creation of investible surpluses was easy in agriculture, their direct mobilisation for productive purposes was difficult. The various methods of mobilisation discussed by him were:

(a) a tax on land revenue or a tax on the area devoted to commercial crops;

(b) intensification of small savings drive;

(c) compulsory delivery of foodgrains; and

(d) tagging of local projects with local resources.

T.M. Joshi and others conducted a study in the taxation of agricultural land and income in India.[22] They found that these two taxes were considerably underplayed as fiscal instruments in the planning process. Despite the great pressure for resource mobilisation for development and defence, the potential of these two taxes remained unexploited.

P.K. Bhargava states that the agricultural sector is relatively lightly taxed and the time has come when greater reliance has to be placed on agricultural and commodity taxation because the possibilities of raising revenue from direct taxes, either by raising their tax rates or extending their coverage are limited.[23] The State governments have to tax the agricultural sector if the tempo of economic development is to be accelerated.

A brief review of studies conducted at the state level is given below:—

Mahesh T. Pathak and Arun S. Patel conducted a comprehensive study of inter-sectoral tax burden for Gujrat.[24] For computing rural and urban shares in indirect taxes (Central and State), a detailed methodology was used to allocate the commodity-wise tax yield among various NSS expenditure groups on the basis of cash expenditure on relevant or related items. A similar study had been made for Uttar Pradesh by the Taxation Enquiry Committee (U.P.).[25] But this study covered only state taxes and one Central tax, viz. income tax. The study also estimated tax incidence for different expenditure groups.

National Council of Applied Economic Research (NCAER) undertook a special income and consumption survey of urban households in Gujrat to estimate tax incidence in the urban sector.[26] The study adopted income rather than expenditure as the basis for calculating tax incidence. Thc amount of different taxes payable by each sample household was calculated by applying the tax rates to the income and expenditure data collected through the survey. The study concluded that while the distribution of tax burden as a whole was progressive with respect to income, that of individual taxes on commodities and services was regressive. The study also tried to estimate the untapped tax potential of the agricultural sector and suggested ways for its mobilization. The levels of net income on farms of more than 20 acres were considered as having the tax potential for yielding additional resources.

A.C. Angrish, on the basis of available data, sought to examine the inter-sectoral tax burden in the State of Rajasthan so as to determine the capacity of the agricultural sector to bear additional taxation.[27] On certain assumptions, he allocated the total direct taxes between the agricultural and non-agricultural sectors in the ratios derived on the basis of the ratio of per capita tax (given by Taxation Enquiry Committee), and population ratio in the state. Considering the combined burden of taxes - direct and indirect - on the two sectors, he also observed that the agricultural sector was lightly taxed compared with non-agricultural sector.

Shyam Nath attempted to measure and analyse the tax incidence on the rural and urban sectors as well as on different expenditure groups in the two sectors in Rajasthan.[28] He took into consideration both direct and indirect taxes levied by the Central and State governments. He found, "At all levels of expenditure, the urban households have borne higher tax incidence than the rural households".

Hemlata Rao probed the inter-sectoral tax burden in U.P. for the period, 1960-61 through 1965-66.[29] She also examined the scope for additional taxation in the agricultural sector in U.P. The analysis showed that tax effort in U.P. had so far been concentrated on the non-agricultural sector. The relative contribution of agriculture to resource mobilisation was insignificant. She took into consideration both direct and indirect taxes of the State and Central governments. She assumed that the yield from Central direct taxes came entirely from the non-agricultural sector. For allocating the incidence of Central indirect taxes (viz. union excise duty) on the agricultural and non-agricultural sectors, she used the NSS data on per capita expenditure on the taxed items. For allocating the burden of state direct taxes, she assumed that the entire sum of land revenue and 20 per cent of the duty on stamps and registration fee fell on agricultural sector. For calculating the ratios of state indirect taxes for the two sectors, she used the percentages of indirect taxes to total expenditure of the respective sectors as given by the U.P. Taxation Enquiry Committee Report (1968-69). Of the state indirect taxes, 57 per cent was borne by the agricultural sector and 43 per cent by the non-agricultural sector. The analysis leads to the common belief that agricultural sector was bearing less total tax burden than the non-agricultural sector.

D.N. Dwivedi worked out the inter-sectoral burden between agricultural and non-agricultural sectors of Uttar Pradesh.[30] He has taken both the direct and indirect taxes imposed by the Central and State governments. His analysis revealed that per capita tax burden in the non-agricultural sector was about seven times higher than that in the agricultural sector. But the difference between the tax-income ratios of the two sectors was not so great. And the marginal increase in the tax burden, on both aggregate and per capita counts, was higher in the agricultural sector than that in the non-agricultural sector. It showed higher rate of progressiveness in the tax burden of the agricultural sector. His assessment for additional agricultural taxation turned out to be

Rs.186.65 crores on the basis of conventional standard of subsistence and Rs.178.35 crores on the basis of nutritional standard.

C.H. Hanumantha Rao calculated the incidence of agricultural taxes (defined as tax/net output ratio) based on the results of field surveys in the three regions of Andhra Pradesh.[31] Rao examined the per acre and per capita impact of land taxes in the selected villages. Further, size-group-wise and crop-wise impact were examined. He also analysed the changes in the impact of agricultural land taxes between 1939 and 1959. On the whole, he observed some fall in the real tax burden over the period. He preferred a progressive land revenue to agricultural income tax on account of simplicity.

Surjit Singh organised a study on certain aspects of agricultural land taxation in Punjab.[32] Jatinder Bhatia also worked out the impact of land taxation according to size of holdings and crops in certain areas of Punjab in 1954-57 and 1961-64.[33]

Sadhu Singh Kahlon examined, in a general way, the land tax structure in Punjab.[34] He opposed the imposition of taxes like estate duty and wealth tax on agricultural land. He supported the view-point that the small farmers be exempted from land tax, though the basis of exemption, according to him should be income rather than land. Relative tax burden on the agricultural sector vis-a-vis non-agricultural sector was, however, not gauged.

J.R. Gupta made a comprehensive study to estimate and analyse the 'tax incidence' and 'expenditure incidence' in Punjab.[35] Whereas inter-sector analysis of tax and expenditure incidence was done for the years 1967-68 to 1976-77, the inter-class analysis was limited only to 1973-74. To study inter-class distribution of tax burden and expenditure benefits, the data pertaining to NSS Consumer Expenditure Survey, 28th Round, 1973-74 were widely used. The main findings of the study are given below.

While the agricultural sector received more benefits from public expenditure, it always bore less burden than the non-agricultural sector. The study covered indirect taxes only. If direct taxes were also taken into account, the inter-sector tax disparity might further accentuate in view of the fact that the non-agricultural sector always bore considerably more direct tax burden than the agricultural sector. The study also measured the taxable capacity of the two sectors and came to the similar conclusion of under-taxation of the agricultural sector.

R.K. Bansal and J.R.Gupta, in their study, investigated the sectoral burden and the distributional effects of sales tax during the period from 1967-68 to 1979-80.[36] On the basis of their analysis, they concluded that the non-agricultural sector was bearing the burden of sales tax in a greater proportion than the agricultural sector. The gap in the per capita sales tax burden as a ratio of per capita income in the respective sectors narrowed down over the period under study. Moreover, sales tax did not appear to have any distributional effect within the agricultural or the non-agricultural sector, but, for the state as a whole, its incidence appeared to be slightly inequitable.

Summing up, the studies considered so far have analysed tax incidence either on the agricultural sector or on the non-agricultural sector or on both. While some of them have been confined to the individual states, others relate to the country as a whole. In spite of the fact that different studies have different coverages, different study periods and different methodologies for calculating tax incidence, they lead more or less to the same conclusion. These studies confirm the existence of untapped tax potential in the agricultural sector and emphasize the need to mop up the same.

Expenditure Benefits

The study of public expenditure like public receipts (i.e. taxes) is significant in order to examine the inter-sector flow of resources.

Fiscal policy is considered a tool not only of resource mobilisation but also to promote production and to influence distribution of income and wealth through public expenditure.

Development policies of the country were hitherto concerned primarily with promoting growth which was viewed as an essential and sufficient pre-condition for an equitable distribution of income. But distribution aspects of development policies have recently acquired new importance. As Robert McNamara puts it, "When the highly privileged are few and the desperately poor are many and when the gap between them is worsening rather than improving, it is only a question of time before a decisive choice must be made between the political costs of reform and the political risks of rebellion".[37]

Luc De Wulf emphasized that most authors who analysed the incidence of government expenditure in developing countries did so in combination with tax incidence estimates, which by themselves did not permit conclusions to be drawn about the redistributional effects of the budget.[38] Similarly, according to D.T. Lakdawala and K.K. Nambias, "Tax burden has its counterpart in expenditure benefits and for a proper judgement of the distributional effect of financial policies both must be considered together".[39]

Richard A. Musgrave and Peggy B. Musgrave also observed, "While taxes impose a burden, this is only one side of the fiscal transactions. To obtain the total picture, the expenditure side of the budget must be considered as well. Since tax revenue is used to provide additional public services, resources are transferred from private to public use and the benefit from the public use must be balanced against the loss of reduced private use. In measuring distributional effects, it will be necessary not only to determine the distribution of tax burden but also that of expenditure benefits and to net out the two".[40]

Thus public expenditure like public receipt is also an important instrument of resource transfer. A number of studies relating to the benefits of public expenditure have been carried out in developing countries in recent years. A few of these analysed the distributional impact of only specific expenditure. Jallade's (1974) study of Colombian Education and Gandhi's (1968) study on the Indian farmers as producers fall in this category.[41] Bird (1970), noting that "It is not conceptually possible to devise a reasonable basis for allocating some expenditure", omitted some items in his expenditure allocation exercise.[42]

In India, a few studies have been conducted to examine the inter-sectoral and inter-class distribution of expenditure benefits. The notable exceptions in this regard were the studies conducted by Ved P. Gandhi and E.T. Mathew.[43] While Gandhi examined the benifits of all public expenditure on revenue account, Mathew confined exclusively to developmental expenditure.

H.M. Groves and M.C. Madhvan made an effort to provide separate estimates for tax and expenditure benefits.[44] They employed an inter-sectoral tax expenditure method to workout the net contribution by the agricultural sector. They used direct and indirect taxes as well as government expenditure for analysis purposes.

K.N. Reddy examined the growth and pattern of government expenditure from 1872 to 1968.[45] To account for territorial changes, the interpretation of estimates was done on per capita basis on the assumption that the territorial changes had not affected per capita estimates. He also classified the public expenditure (both on revenue account and capital account) into two heads viz. developmental and non-developmental.

Zahir Mohammad scrutinized the pattern of public expenditure with a different objective.[46] His main aim was to study the impact of public expenditure on people's income distribution. He studied income and wealth distribution in India and also analysed inflation as well as the pattern of income distribution.

K.N. Reddy's study of fiscal burden covered expenditure benefits of both the Central and the State Governments.[47] Further, he considered the expenditure on revenue account both at the Central and State levels. In so far as expenditure on capital account was considered, the study was confined to development expenditure only.

E.T. Mathew worked out the net burden of agricultural

taxation in India by substracting negative taxes (i.e. benefits enjoyed by the tax-payers) from positive ones (i.e. taxes in ordinary sense).[48] The budgets of the Central and State governments consist of two parts, revenue account and capital account. Expenditure on revenue account is supposed to be met from current revenue. Expenditure in the nature of an investment are not included in the revenue account. On the other hand, expenditures on capital account are not usually met from current revenue. Expenditure on revenue account benefits the recipients immediately, whereas those on the capital account take time for fruition. Mathew took into consideration only the relevant social and developmental expenditures on the revenue account, such as agriculture and rural development, irrigation, multipurpose river valley schemes, veterinary services, community projects, national extension service and local development works, education and medical and public health services.

J.R. Gupta's study analyses inter-sector expenditure incidence for the years 1967-68 to 1976-77; the inter-class analysis has been done only for 1973-74.[49] He has worked out the incidence of developmental expenditure on revenue account but has left out the incidence of non-developmental and capital expenditures. The study concludes that the agricultural sector has always received more benefits from public expenditure than those from non-agricultural sector. He further concludes that the fact that the agricultural sector is under-taxed is true in relation to the expenditure benefits it has received, as also when the taxable capacity of the two sectors is considered.

In the end, we can conclude that though most of the studies concentrated on the distribution of tax burden, for a balanced view of the distribution of fiscal burden, the study of the distiribution of benefits of public expenditure assumes significance.

REFERENCES

1. R.J. Chelliah, *Fiscal Policy in Underdeveloped Countries with Special reference to India,* (George Allen and Unwin Ltd., London 1969), p. 66.
2. Government of India, Ministry of Finance, *Taxation Enquiry*

Commission Report, 1953-54, (New Delhi, Vol. 1 1955), p. 46.

3. *Ibid.*
4. Government of India, Ministry of Finance, *Incidence of Indirect Taxation, 1958-59,* (New Delhi, 1960).
5. Government of India, Ministry of Finance, *Incidence of Indirect Taxation, 1963-64,* (New Delhi, 1969).
6. K.N. Raj, "Resources for the Third Plan—An Approach", *Economic Weekly,* Annual Number (Vol. XI, January, 1959), pp. 203-208.
7. E.T. Mathew, *Agricultural Taxation and Economic Development in India,* (Bombay, Asia Publishing House, 1968).
8. Ved. P. Gandhi, *Tax Burden in Indian Agriculture* (Combridge, The Law School of Harvard University, 1966).
9. Ved. P. Gandhi, *Some Aspects of India's Tax Structure,* (Bombay, Vora and Company, 1970).
10. H.F. Lydall and M. Ahmed, "An Exercise in Forecasting Consumer Demand and Taxation Yields in India in 1965-66", *Indian Economic Review,* (August 1961).
11. S.L. Shetty, "An Inter-Sectoral Analysis of Taxable Capacity and Tax Burden", *Indian Journal of Agricultural Economics* (Vol. XXVI, No. 3, July-Sept. 1971). pp. 216-246.
12. S.L. Shetty, "Inter-Class Incidence of Taxation in Farm and Non-Farm Sectors in India", *Economic and Political Weekly,* (Review of Agriculture, Vol. VI, No. 2, December 25, 1971). pp. A-173 to A-186.
13. K.S.R.N. Sarma and M.J.K. Thavaraj, "Estimation of Tax Incidence in India", *Economic and Political Weekly,* (Vol. VI, No. 19, May 8, 1971), pp. 957-964.
14. (a) Ved P. Gandhi, *op.cit.*

    (b) E.T. Mathew, *op.cit.*
15. K.N. Reddy, *Tax Burden on Agriculture in India; An Enquiry into the Feasibility of Agricultural Income Tax* (Baroda, Good Companions Publishers, 1972).
16. The Economic Times Research Bureau, "Tax Potential of Farm Income", *The Economic Times,* (Annual 1974), pp. 142-153.
17. Government of India, Ministry of Finance, *Report of the Indirect Taxation Enquiry Committeee* (New Delhi, October 1977 and January 1978, Vols. I and II).

18. Raja J. Chelliah and Ram N. Lal, *Incidence of Indirect Taxation in India 1973-74,* (New Delhi, National Institute of Public Finance and Policy, 1978).
19. T. Divakara Rao, *Tax Burden in Indian Economy,* (New Delhi, Criterion Publications, 1984).
20. S.S. Johl, "Agricultural Taxation in a Developing Economy : A Case of India", *Indian Journal of Agricultural Economics,* (Vol. 27, No. 3, July-September 1972). pp. 1-19.
21. N.A. Khan, "Resource Mobilization from Agriculture and Economic Development in India", *Economic Development and Cultural Change,* (Vol. 2, Oct. 1963), pp. 42-54.
22. T.M. Joshi, et. al., *Studies in Taxation of Agricultural Land and Income in India,* (London, Asia Publishing House, 1968).
23. P.K. Bhargava, *Some Aspects of Indian Public Ficance,* (New Delhi, Uppal Publishing House (1984).
24. Mahesh T. Pathak and Arun S. Patel, *Agricultural Taxation in Gujarat,* (Bombay, Asia Publishing House, 1968).
25. Uttar Pradesh, *Taxation Enquiry Committee Report, 1968-69, (Lucknow 1969).*
26. NCAER, *Incidence of Taxation in Gujarat,* (New Delhi 1970).
27. A.C. Angrish, "Agricultural and Non-Agricultural Taxation : An Estimate of Their Burden in Rajasthan", *Economic and Political Weekly,* (Vol. V, No. 2, January 10, 1970), pp. 59-66.
28. Shyam Nath, "Incidence of Taxation in Rajasthan", *Margin,* (Vol. 12, No. 3, April 1980), pp. 60-73.
29. Hemlata Rao, "Tax Incidence on Agricultural Sector in Uttar Pradesh", *Economic and Political Weekly,* (Vol. VI, No. 37, September 11, 1971), pp. 1961-1968.
30. D.N. Dwivedi, *Problems and Prospects of Agricultural Taxation in U.P.* (New Delhi, People's Publishing House, January 1973).
31. C.H. Hanumantha Rao, *Taxation of Agricultural Land in Andhra Pradesh,* (Bombay, Asia Publishing House, 1962).
32. Surjit Singh, *A Study of Certain Aspects of Agricultural Land Taxation in the State of Punjab (India),* (Okahoma State University, U.S.A. 1965) Ph.D. Thesis, Unpublished.
33. Jatinder Bhatia, " Agricultural Land Taxation in Punjab" *Economic and Political Weekly,* (Vol IX, No. 3, January 18, 1969), pp. 211-215.
34. Sadhu Singh Kahlon, *Land Tax Structure in Punjab, An Analytical*

Study, (Ludhiana, Punjab Agricultural University 1975) Unpublished.

35. J.R. Gupta, *Burden of Tax in Punjab - An Inter-sectoral and Inter-class Analysis,* (New Delhi, Concept Publishing Company, 1983).
36. R.K. Bansal and J.R. Gupta, *Economic Aspects of Sales Tax : A Case Study of Punjab,* (New Delhi, Atlantic Publishers and Distributors, 1985).
37. Robert McNamara, as quoted in Luc De Wulf, "Fiscal Incidence Strdies in Developing Countries : Survey and Technique", *IMF Staff Papers,* (Vol. XXII, No. 1, March 1975), pp. 61-131.
38. Luc De Wulf, *op.cit.,* p. 75.
39. D.T. Lakdawala and K.V. Nambias, *Commodity Taxation in India,* (Ahmedabad, Sardar Patel Institute of Economics and Social Research, 1972), pp. 31-32.
40. Richard A. Musgrave and Peggy B. Musgrave, *Public Finance in Theory and Practice,* (New York, McGraw Hill Book Company 1973), p. 357.
41. As quoted in Luc De Wulf, "Fiscal Incidence Studies in Developing Countries", *IMF Staff Papers,* (Vol. 22, No. 1, March 1975) pp. 61-131.
42. *Ibid.*
43. (a) Ved P. Gandhi, *Tax Burden in Indian Agriculture,* (Cambridge, The Law School of Harvard University, 1966).
    (b) E.T. Mathew, *op.cit.*
44. H.M. Groves and M.C. Madhvan, "Agricultural Taxation and India's Third Five-Year Plan", *Land Economics* (Vol. 38, No. 1, 1962), pp. 57-59.
45. K.N. Reddy, *The Growth of Public Expenditure in India,* (Delhi, Sterling Publishers (P) Ltd., 1972).
46. Zahir Mohammad, *Public Expenditure and Income Distribution in India* (New Delhi, Associated Publishing House, 1972).
47. K.N. Reddy, *Tax Burden on Agriculture in India,* (An Inquiry into the Feasibility of Agricultural Income Tax), (Baroda, Good Companions Publishers, 1972).
48. E.T. Methew, *op.cit.*
49. J.R. Gupta, *op.cit.*

PART C

6

Agricultural Surplus and its Mobilization: A Case Study of Punjab

LEON Walras whom Joseph Schumpeter describes as "the greatest of all economists" conceives economics as a rational and empirical science in which both reason and experience play their roles. To be useful, a concept cannot be just a bloodless abstraction; it must be capable of being tested empirically. The preceding discussion focused, in the main, on agricultural surplus as a theoretical construct, as also on the prime instruments through which this surplus can be mobilized. The purpose of the present chapter is to test the concept empirically. This exercise has been carried out with respect to a large volume of data from Punjab which has experienced profound and sweeping changes in its agricultural sector, graphically described by the term "Green Revolution".

The analysis is based on secondary data for fifteen years beginning 1967-68. This was considered an appropriate base in view of the fact that the present Punjab came into being in 1966 when the region was territorially reorganized.

The investigation is addressed to three major concerns:

one, whether the various concepts of agricultural surplus as outlined in Chapter 2 are workable;

two, which one of the concepts is rather suitable to measure the magnitude of agricultural surplus; and

three, to find out, if any agricultural surplus is available.

For estimating potential surplus in both agricultural and non-agricultural sectors of Punjab, the following four approximations were used.

$$\text{Potential Surplus} = (Y - C_m)\,P \qquad \text{(I)}$$

where Y = Income per head,

C_m = Minimum consumption per head,

P = Population.

In the first approximation, the most elusive is the concept of minimum consumption requirements. It depends on so many factors that it is difficult to signify the quantum of consumption requirements. However, in the present study, the calorie norms of K.L. Datta estimated for Punjab (both in rural and urban sectors) have been used after making due allowances for price changes.

The estimation of potential surplus, particularly at the inter-sector level, must make allowances for investment. Therefore, equation (I) gets modified as:

$$\text{Potential Surplus} = (Y - C_m)\,P - I_m \qquad \text{(II)}$$

where I_m = Minimum investment requirements.

Both these approximations were based on the assumption that minimum consumption requirements per person were uniformally applicable to the entire population. But, in reality there might be a considerable number of households whose actual consumption might be less than the estimated minimum requirements. The extent of potential surplus will be different while taking into account actual consumption. This is shown in equation (III).

$$\text{Potential Surplus} = Y - (C_a\,P_1 + C_m\,P_2) \qquad \text{(III)}$$

where P_1 = Population whose actual consumption was less than the estimated minimum consumption,

P_2 = Population whose actual consumption was more than the estimated minimum consumption,

C_a = Actual per capita consumption of households with P_1 population, and

C_m= Estimated per capita minimum consumption of households with P_2 population.

In equation (III), if we make allowances for minimum investment requirements, we will get the fourth equation as follows:

$$\text{Potential Surplus} = Y - (C_a P_1 + C_m P_2) - I_m \qquad \text{(IV)}$$

The potential surpluses based on these four approximations have been summed up in Tables 6.1 to 6.5.

For mobilizing surpluses, the present study has focused on the following specific methods:

(i) changing terms of trade;

(ii) effecting changes in the administrative prices and mobilizing marketed / marketable surpluses; and

(iii) diverting financial resources, using taxation and expenditure policies.

The inter-sector analysis of distribution of tax burden and expenditure benefits has been done for the years 1967-68 through 1981-82. Based on the data pertaining to the National Sample Survey (NSS) Consumer Expenditure Survey (32nd Round, 1977-78), the inter-class analysis of tax burden and expenditure benefits has been done for one year only (1977-78). Different expenditure groups have been identified as various economic classes. Simple techniques like compound growth rates, buoyancy co-efficients and concentration ratios have been used for purposes of quantitative analysis. For examining the distribution of tax burden, the important state taxes considered are: State excise duty, sales tax, motor vehicles tax, stamp duty and registration fee, electricity duty, entertainment tax, passenger and goods tax and land revenue. On the expenditure side, only development expenditure on revenue account has been analysed. The expenditure items for which benefits have been analysed are education, medical and public health services, transport, agriculture, industry, co-operation and other items which include civil works and multi-purpose river valley schemes.

To examine the re-distributional effects of tax burden and expenditure benefits, concentration ratios were worked out for the proportions of consumer expenditure vis-a-vis proportions of population as revealed in the 32nd Round of NSS Consumer Expenditure Survey. For calculating concentration ratio, the following formula was used:

$$C = \sum_{i=2}^{n} P_{i-1} Q_i - \sum_{i=2}^{n} Pi\, Q_{i-1}$$

where C is the co-efficient of concentration and P and Q are cumulative percentages.

Findings

Major findings of the study for the State of Punjab are as follows:—

(1) Based on different assumptions, it was found that potential surpluses existed in both agricultural and non-agricultural sectors of Punjab (Tables 6.1 to 6.4). The per capita potential surplus (in absolute terms as well as percentage of per capita income) was higher in the agricultural sector than that in the non-agricultural sector for the first three or four years of the study period and the reverse was the case for the rest of the years. The ratios of per capita potential surplus of the agricultural sector to those of the non-agricultural sector were on the decline as potrayed in Table 6.5. The reason for this decline appears to be that both income and potential surplus per capita in the non-agricultural sector were increasing at a higher rate than those in the agricultural sector.

(2) The movements in index numbers of parity (i.e. the ratio of prices received by the farmers to prices paid by the farmers) were also analysed. The index number of parity prepared by the Economic Adviser to the State government with 1959-62 as the base was re-constructed, taking 1967-68 through 1969-70 as the

base (Table 6.6). The data presented in Tablc 6.6 revealed that, out of 14 years considered (from 1967-68 to 1980-81), the terms of trade were found to be favourable to the agricultural sector for five years only (i.e. 1967-68, 1973-74, 1974-75, 1978-79 and 1980-81). The linear trend line fitted showed that the parity indices were falling at a marginal rate of 0.02 per annum but this fall was not statistically significant.

(3) The data pertaining to parity indices for the post-harvest prices of seven major crops viz. wheat, paddy, cotton (American), barley, bajra, maize and gram in relation to the wholesale prices of (a) 50 agricultural commodities and (b) 21 agricultural commodities have been shown in Tables 6.7 and 6.8. The analysis pointed out that the indices of parity were mostly below unity for wheat, barley and bajra for most of the years. These indices of parity turned out to be favourable for paddy (initial years), cotton (American), gram and maize and unfavourable for wheat, barley and bajra. Thus the crops for which the indices were fovourable were those whose importance was diminishing. Wheat and paddy were two crops for which indices were unfavourable and they occupied the highest proportion of area which further expanded between 1967-68 and 1981-82.

(4) Table 6.9 contains information regarding shifts in sectoral income. The data showing differences between the current price income and constant price income of both the sectors over a period of time highlighted that there was a transfer of Rs. 14,619.3 millions from agricultural to non-agricultural sector owing to the movement of relative prices for the period 1970-71 through 1981-82.

(5) Table 6.10 provides information on production vis-a-vis marketed surplus in the case of three major crops of Punjab viz. wheat, paddy and maize. The proportion of marketed surplus to total production rose for wheat

from 48.2 per cent in 1967-68 to 57.3 in 1981-82 and for paddy from 60.6 per cent to 91.84 per cent. However, for maize, the market arrivals as percentage of production dropped from 36.4 per cent in 1967-68 to 5.92 per cent in 1981-82.

(6) Table 6.11 displays data on the market arrivals of wheat and rice for different time periods. The data indicate that the percentage distributions of market arrivals of wheat and rice were quite different in 1978-79 and 1979-80 from those in 1961-62. The pattern of market arrivals changed significantly. There were heavy market arrivals of these crops in the immediate post-harvest season.

(7) The data in Table 6.12 give information regarding production and procurement of two major crops, namely wheat and rice. In the case of wheat, the share of procurement in output fluctuated between 20.34 per cent and 59.07 per cent during the period from 1967-68 to 1981-82. Punjab's share in national procurement of wheat also varied between 73.17 per cent in 1967-68 and 57.17 per cent in 1981-82. In the case of rice, the percentage of procurement of production rose from 54.68 per cent in 1968-69 to 75.39 per cent in 1981-82. Thus, it is extremely relevant to point out that the surpluses of wheat and rice in Punjab brought increased incomes to their producers primarily because of government price support policy, accompanied by bulk purchases to sustain the national network of buffer stocks.

(8) Profitability of wheat measured as the difference between the procurement price and the cost of production per quintal has been exhibited in Table 6.13. On 'A_2'* cost basis, the profitability of wheat in money

* 'A_2'cost covers paid-out expenses on material-inputs, hired human labour, bullock and machine labour expenses and rent paid for leased-in land.

terms shot up from Rs. 40.63 in 1967-68 to Rs. 66.81 in 1981-82, the corresponding increase on 'C'* cost basis was from Rs. 20.98 to Rs. 23.23. On the other hand, on 'A_2' cost basis, the profitability of wheat in real terms sank from Rs. 40.63 in 1967-68 to Rs. 26 in 1981-82, the corresponding decline on 'C' cost basis was from Rs. 20.98 to Rs. 9.04. In the case of paddy, per quintal net return over 'C' cost in money terms turned out to be negative for three years (i.e. 1971-72, 1974-75 and 1975-76). However, after 1975-76, net returns in money as well as real terms were showing an increasing trend.

(9) The data regarding taxation as an important tool of resource mobilization have been presented in Table 6.14. Tax revenue in the State constituted about 64.35 per cent of total revenue in 1967-68 and 82.03 per cent in 1981-82. Among the State's taxes, sales tax made the largest contribution (36.58 per cent), followed by State excise duty (22.13 per cent), stamp duty and registration fee (8.91 per cent), passenger and goods tax (6.21 per cent), motor vehicles tax (3.1 per cent), entertainment tax (1.94 per cent), land revenue (0.61 per cent), and others (0.02 per cent) in 1981-82. The behaviour of tax system was also examined with the help of compound growth rates and buoyancy co-efficients. The compound growth rate for the period under study came out to be maximum for motor vehicles tax (21.89 per cent), followed by sales tax (17.7 per cent), entertainment tax (17.55 per cent), electriciy duty (16.74 per cent), passenger and goods tax (15.59 per cent), stamp duty and registration fee (14.77 per cent), State excise duty (14.41 per cent), and land revenue (4.94 per cent). The co-efficients of buoyancy were more than unity for all taxes other than land revenue and estate duty.

---

* 'C' cost includes both paid-out as well as imputed and rising cost on account of family's own resources.

(10) Table 6.15 presents data on the distribution of per capita burden of State taxes (viz., land revenue, sales tax, State excise duty, passenger and goods tax, motor vehicles tax, stamp duty and registration fee, electricity duty, and entertainment tax). The data in the table showed that, while for some taxes (viz. land revenue, State excise duty and passenger and goods tax), the burden was higher on the agricultural sector; for other taxes (viz., sales tax, motor vehicles tax, stamp duty and registration fee, electricity duty and entertainment tax), the burden was higher on the non-agricultural sector. The total per capita tax burden on the agricultural sector sky-rocketed from Rs. 36.73 in 1967-68 to Rs. 229.62 in 1981-82, the corresponding increase for the non-agricultural sector was from Rs. 39.26 to Rs. 285.91. Thus not only the total per capita tax burden (in absolute terms) was more in the case of the non-agricultural sector than that on the agricultural sector but the gap was also found to be widening over the period under study. The ratio of the tax burden of the agricultural sector to that of the non-agricultural sector (in absolute terms) shrank from 0.94 in 1967-68 to 0.8 in 1981-82.

(11) Table 6.15 presenting data for the per capita inter-sector distribution of tax burden in relation to the per capita inter-sector income brought to light a very significant trend in real tax burden. The ratio of per capita income of the agricultural sector to that of the non-agricultural sector was higher for about six years than the ratio of their respective tax burdens during the entire study period. Consequently, the ratio of relative tax burden (defined as tax burden in relation to sectoral income) was lower for the agricultural sector for six years and higher for the remaining period.

(12) The data in Table 6.16 reflect an inter-class analysis of tax burden in the agricultural sector for one year

only i.e. for 1977-78. It is clear from the table that the per capita burden of all the taxes except stamp duty and registration fee moved up as we moved from the lowest expenditure group to the highest expenditure group. Among the taxes considered, sales tax and State excise duty were the main sources of tax revenue in respect of all the expenditure groups. Next in importance was the passenger tax whose burden increased from Rs. 2.48 per capita for the lowest expenditure group to Rs. 30.51 per capita for the highest expenditure group. The per capita burden of all the taxes taken together increased from Rs. 20.79 in the case of the lowest expenditure group to Rs. 484.29 in the case of the highest expenditure group.

(13) Table 6.17 depicts per capita burden of all taxes on non-agricultural sector for different expenditure groups. Per capita burden of sales tax proved to be predominant for all the expenditure groups. The burden of all the taxes (except stamp duty and registration fee) increased as we moved from the lowest to the highest expenditure groups. Per capita burden of all the taxes taken together zoomed up from Rs. 43.92 to Rs. 595.87 as we moved from the lowest to the highest expenditure groups. Thus, all the expenditure groups (except expenditure group with per capita monthly consumption expenditure of Rs. 150-200) in the non-agricultural sector carried higher per capita burdens than their counterparts in the agricultural sector.

(14) Table 6.18 represents data on per capita tax burden for the State as a whole. Here again sales tax and State excise duty seemed to hold the key positions. The per capita burden of all the taxes taken together climbed up consistently from Rs. 29.2 to Rs. 536 as we climbed from the lowest to the highest expenditure groups.

(15) The data pertaining to per capita tax burden in relation to per capita cash expenditure/total expenditure marked an upward trend (except for stamp duty and registration fee) in the agricultural sector and regressive tendency in the non-agricultural sector, moving from the lowest to the highest expenditure groups. For the State as a whole, upward trends were observed except for electricity duty.

(16) In order to examine the distributional implications of different taxes, concentration ratios for the proportions of consumption expenditure (vis-a-vis the proportions of population) before and after paying the taxes were estimated and chalked out in Table 6.19 through 6.21. The distributional impact of taxes was observed to be somewhat positive in the agricultural sector and negative in the non-agricultural sector. The concentration ratio for consumption expenditure slid down from 0.2378 to 0.2199 for the agricultural sector and went up from 0.2504 to 0.3138 for the non-agricultural sector when the tax burden was taken into account. For the State as a whole, this ratio dwindled from 0.2456 to 0.2296. Thus, the agricultural sector had a markedly predominent influence when the distributional implications of the tax burden were considered.

Some findings regarding expenditure side of the budget are given below:—

(17) The State incurred two types of expenditure: (a) expenditure on revenue account and (b) expenditure on capital account. Table 6.22 incorporates data on the growth of public expenditure on revenue account in Punjab. Whereas total receipts under revenue account surged up from Rs. 10,545.42 lakhs to Rs. 68,261.4 lakhs, total expenditure on revenue account registered an increase from Rs. 9,683.79 lakhs to Rs. 61,998.21 lakhs during the study period. Thus,

there has always been a surplus on revenue account. In 1981-82, development expenditurc on revenue account formed about 69.41 per cent of the total expenditure and non-development expenditure about 30.59 per cent.

(18) Table 6.23 contains information on distribution of benefits from different items of development expenditure. The expenditure on education had top priority in the total development expenditure. Its share was maximum (i.e. 37.21 per cent) in 1968-69 and minimum (28.47 per cent) in 1972-73. The relative share of transport and communication rose from 7.71 per cent in 1967-68 to 18.11 per cent in 1981-82. Medical and public health also constituted an important source of development expenditure. Its relative share slightly swelled from 10.39 per cent in 1967-68 to 13.72 per cent in 1981-82. The relative share of agriculture and allied services declined sharply from 25.78 per cent to 14.77 per cent during the study period. The compound growth rate turned out to be the highest in the case of transport and communication (23.85 per cent), followed by medical and public health (17.38 per cent), others (16.28 per cent), education (14.78 per cent), cooperation (14.57 per cent), agriculture (10.3 per cent) and industry (7.93 per cent). The co-efficients of buoyancy were more than unity for all the items of development expenditure except agriculture and industry where these co-efficients were 0.81 and 0.64 respectively.

(19) Table 6.24 manifests data regarding inter-sectoral per capita benefits from different items of development expenditure over the period under study. The table revealed that per capita benefits from education were less in the agricultural sector than those in the non-agricultural sector up to the period 1972-73 and the reverse was the case for rest of the period. More per capita benefits were enjoyed by the agricultural sector

than by the non-agricultural sector in the case of transport, agriculture and co-operation. In the case of expenditure on medical and public health and that on industry, the non-agricultural sector was in a better position than the agricultural sector for the period under study.

(20) The data on inter-sector distribution of per capita benefits (Table 6.25) illustrated that these rose (in absolute terms) from Rs. 50.07 to Rs. 292.94 for the agricultural sector and from Rs.38.07 to Rs.179.35 for the non-agricultural sector during the period 1967-68 through 1981-82. In other words, the combined benefits from all types of development expenditure were found to be more in agricultural sector throughout the study period. Further, the ratio of per capita benefits to per capital income jumped up from 5.88 per cent in 1967-68 to 11.59 per cent in 1981-82 in the case of the agricultural sector; it coursed downward from 4.73 per cent to 3.68 per cent in the case of the non-agricultural sector. For the State as a whole, it soared from 5.47 per cent in 1967-68 to 7.1 per cent in 1981-82. The inter-sector ratio of per capita benefits to per capita income spiralled up from 1.24 in 1967-68 to 3.15 in 1981-82, thereby showing more benefits enjoyed by the agricultural sector than by the non-agricultural sector.

The major findings of the study of inter-class distribution of benefits from public expenditure in Punjab are outlined below.

(21) Tables 6.26 and 6.27 encapsulate data on per capita benefits from different items of expenditure for different expenditure groups in the agricultural and non-agricultural sector, respectively. Per capita benefits on education, medical and public health, as also from transport, were found to be improving from the lowest to the highest expenditure groups in both the sectors. Total benefits from development

expenditure multiplied from Rs. 61.75 to Rs. 309.21 in the agricultural sector and from Rs. 42.44 to Rs. 222.10 in the non-agricultural sector as one moved from the lowest to the highest expenditure groups. It is also clear from these tables that total expenditure benefits (excluding agricultural and industrial development expenditure) enjoyed by all classes in the agricultural sector were more than those enjoyed by their counterparts in the non-agricultural sector.

(22) The data in Table 6.28 for the State of Punjab as a whole pin-pointed an upward trend in the distribution of benefits from individual items of development expenditure (barring a few deviations) as one moved from the lowest to the highest expenditure groups.

(23) Tables 6.29 and 6.30 sum up the data on the distribution of per capita benefits in relation to per capita expenditure for different expenditure groups in agricultural and non-agricultural sectors, respectively. It is evident from these tables that all the expenditure groups in the agricultural sector enjoyed more benefits than their counterparts in the non-agricultural sector.

(24) Tables 6.31 through 6.33 examine the re-distributional effect of public expenditure. The distribution of expenditure benefits, excluding those from agricultural development expenditure, in the agricultural sector appeared to have somewhat moderating influence on the inter-personal inequalities in the distribution of consumption expenditure. The concentration ratio slipped down from 0.2378 to 0.223 when expenditure benefits were included.

In the case of the non-agricultural sector, also, the concentration ratio of consumption expenditure contracted from 0.2504 to 0.233 when the expenditure benefits were considered.

For the State as a whole, the concentration ratio was reduced from 0.2456 to 0.2256 when expenditure benefits were taken into account. Thus the expenditure benefits were found to have somewhat moderating influence to correct the distributional inequalities.

(25) Table 6.34 indicates that per capita benefits of each expenditure group went up further after including agricultural and industrial development expenditure in the case of both the sectors.

(26) The results of per capita benefits (including agricultural development and industrial development expenditure) in relation to per capita expenditure supported the conclusion that different groups in the agricultural sector continued to enjoy more benefits than their counterparts in the non-agricultural sector (Table 6.35).

(27) The data in Table 6.36 indicate the re-distributional effects of public expenditure, including agricultural and industrial development expenditure. In the case of the agricultural sector, the concentration ratio of consumption expenditure plunged from 0.223 to 0.1903 when benefits from agricultural development expenditure were also considered.

In the case of non-agricultural sector, the distribution of consumption expenditure, inclusive of expenditure benefits, became a little more inequitable when industrial development expenditure was brought under focus. The concentration ratio slightly mounted from 0.233 to 0.2352 when benefits from industrial development expenditure were taken into account.

However, for the State as a whole, this ratio crashed from 0.2256 to 0.203 when benefits, both from agricultural and industrial development expenditure, were accounted for.

To summarize, it may be stated that per capita potential surpluses exist both in the agricultural and non-agricultural sectors of the State. Moreover, because of rapid increase in per capita income of the non-agricultural sector in recent years, the potential surpluses have increased at a much higher rate in this sector than those in the agricultural sector. Besides, the agricultural sector has also been deprived of some resources through adverse terms of trade. The State's agriculture has come to specialise in the production of wheat and rice, the major proportions of which are purchased for the Central pool at fixed procurement prices. In the case of wheat, though profitability, defined as the difference between the procurement price and the cost of production, has increased in money terms, a perceptible fall has been observed in real terms. For paddy, however, profitability, both in money and real terms, has upswing in recent years in spite of the fact that it was negative in the initial years of the study. The ratios of post-harvest prices to wholesale prices of fifty agricultural and non-agricultural commodities have almost been unfavourable all through in the case of wheat. In the case of paddy, also, these ratios have become unfavourable, particularly after 1973-74. The analysis of shifts in the sectoral income has revealed that over the period 1970-71 through 1981-82, a net transfer of Rs.14,619.3 millions from the agricultural to the non-agricultural sectors has taken place.

The distribution of tax burden between the two sectors showed that, though in absolute terms the agricultural sector has been bearing less burden than the non-agricultural sector, yet in relation to the sectors income the agricultural sector bore less burden only up to 1974-75, whereafter the scales seemed to have turned against it. The distribution of tax burden within the sector broughtout that while it had a somewhat positive effect on reducing inequalities in the agricultural sector, the reverse was the case for the non-agricultural sector.

The inter-sectoral distribution of benefits of public expenditure spotlighted that the agricultural sector had been favoured all through the period. The distribution of such benefits within the agricultural sector revealed that the thrust of public expenditure was clearly on reducing disparities. Thus, it is a happy augury that the tax and expenditure policies of the State Government have been formulated to serve the broadest objective of achieving equality by strengthening the weaker groups. It will be a welcome step if such policies are extended to the non-agricultural sector as well.

Table 6.1: Growth of Potential Surplus in the A and N Sectors in Punjab (First Approximation)

Years	*A Sector*				*N Sector*				*Ratio of (5) to (9)*
	Per capita income (Rs.)	*Per capita minimum consumption (Rs.)*	*Per capita potential surplus (Rs.)*	*(4) as percentage of (2)*	*Per capita income (Rs.)*	*Per capita minimum consumption (Rs.)*	*Per capita potential surplus (Rs.)*	*(8) as percentage of (6)*	
1	2	3	4	5	6	7	8	9	10
1967-68	851.30	468.59	302.71	44.96	825.37	518.09	307.28	37.23	1.21
1968-69	915.76	461.33	454.43	49.62	907.24	504.83	402.41	44.35	1.12
1969-70	977.20	473.42	503.78	51.55	980.45	532.13	448.32	45.73	1.13
1970-71	1003.02	468.59	534.78	53.28	1101.57	521.82	579.75	52.63	1.01
1971-72	1043.98	492.72	551.26	52.80	1167.20	525.24	641.96	55.00	0.96
1972-73	1115.87	526.55	589.32	52.81	1289.74	588.91	700.83	54.34	0.97
1973-74	1474.02	659.40	814.62	55.26	1406.91	733.20	673.71	47.88	1.15
1974-75	1514.93	813.99	700.94	46.27	1565.97	940.95	625.02	39.91	1.16
1975-76	1487.27	743.93	743.34	49.98	2202.38	880.44	1321.94	60.02	0.83
1976-77	1742.65	736.72	1005.93	57.72	2494.36	835.88	1658.48	66.49	0.87
1977-78	1876.27	801.90	1074.37	57.26	2827.16	979.40	1847.76	65.36	0.88
1978-79	1921.65	804.33	1117.32	58.14	3059.59	956.60	2102.99	68.73	0.85
1979-80	2086.52	903.35	1183.17	56.70	3465.16	1105.65	2359.51	68.09	0.83
1980-81	2086.10	1055.55	1030.55	49.40	3888.21	1346.56	2541.65	65.37	0.75
1981-82	2527.02	1120.73	1406.29	55.65	4867.52	1458.52	3409.31	70.04	0.79

Note : A stands for agricultural sector.
N stands for non-agricultural sector.

Tabele 6.2: Growth of Potential Surplus in the A and N Sectors in Punjab (Second Approximation)

Years	*A Sector*				*N Sector*				*Ratio of (5) to (8)*
	Per capita income (Rs.)	*Per capita minimum consumption plus minimum investment (Rs.)*	*Per capita potential surplus (Rs.)*	*(4) as percentage of (2)*	*Per capita income (Rs.)*	*Per capita minimum consumption plus minimum investment (Rs.)*	*Per capita potential surplus (Rs.)*	*(8) as percentage of (6)*	
1	2	3	4	5	6	7	8	9	10
1967-68	851.30	537.46	313.84	36.87	825.37	623.41	201.96	24.47	1.51
1968-69	915.76	535.41	380.35	41.53	907.24	620.59	286.65	31.60	1.31
1969-70	977.20	552.48	424.72	43.46	980.45	657.23	323.22	32.97	1.32
1970-71	1003.02	549.73	453.29	45.19	1101.57	662.38	439.19	39.87	1.13
1971-72	1043.98	577.18	466.80	44.71	1167.20	674.17	493.03	42.24	1.06
1972-73	1115.87	616.82	499.05	44.72	1289.74	753.48	536.26	41.58	1.08
1973-74	1474.02	778.65	695.37	47.17	1406.91	912.72	494.19	35.13	1.34
1974-75	1514.93	936.55	578.38	38.18	1565.97	1140.77	425.20	27.15	1.41
1975-76	1487.27	864.25	623.02	41.89	2202.38	1161.46	1040.92	47.26	0.89
1976-77	1742.65	877.70	864.95	49.63	2494.36	1154.16	1340.20	53.73	0.92
1977-78	1876.27	953.69	922.58	49.17	2827.16	1340.15	1487.01	52.60	0.93
1978-79	1921.65	959.79	961.86	50.05	3059.59	1347.00	1712.59	55.97	0.89
1979-80	2086.52	1072.15	1014.37	48.61	3465.16	1547.80	1917.36	55.33	0.88
1980-81	2086.10	1224.31	861.79	41.31	3888.21	1842.69	2045.52	52.61	0.78
1981-82	2527.02	1325.17	1201.85	47.56	4867.52	2079.30	2788.22	57.28	0.83

Note : A stands for agricultural sector.
N stands for non-agricultural sector.

Table 6.3: Growth of Potential Surplus in the A and N Sectors in Punjab (Third Approximation)

Years	*A Sector*				*N Sector*				*Ratio of (5) to (9)*
	Per capita income (Rs.)	*Per capita minimum consumption (Rs.)*	*Potential surplus (Rs.)*	*(4) as percentage of (2)*	*Per capita income (Rs.)*	*Per capita minimum consumption (Rs.)*	*Potential surplus (Rs.)*	*(8) as percentage of (6)*	
1	2	3	4	5	6	7	8	9	10
1967-68	851.30	440.79	410.51	48.22	825.37	468.85	356.52	43.19	1.12
1968-69	915.76	433.96	481.80	52.61	907.24	456.85	450.39	49.64	1.06
1969-70	977.20	445.33	531.87	54.43	980.45	481.56	498.89	50.88	1.07
1970-71	1003.02	440.79	562.23	56.05	1101.57	472.23	629.34	57.13	0.98
1971-72	1043.98	463.49	580.49	55.60	1167.20	475.32	691.88	59.28	0.94
1972-73	1115.87	495.31	620.56	55.61	1289.74	532.94	756.94	58.68	0.95
1973-74	1474.02	620.28	853.74	57.92	1406.91	663.52	743.39	52.84	1.10
1974-75	1514.93	765.69	749.24	49.46	1565.97	851.53	714.44	45.44	1.08
1975-76	1487.27	699.79	787.48	52.95	2202.38	796.77	1405.61	63.82	0.83
1776-77	1742.65	693.01	1049.64	60.23	2494.36	756.45	1737.91	69.67	0.86
1977-78	1876.27	754.32	1121.95	59.80	2827.16	886.32	1940.84	58.65	0.87
1978-79	1921.65	756.61	1165.04	60.63	3059.59	865.69	2193.90	71.71	0.84
1979-80	2086.52	849.75	1236.77	59.27	3465.16	1000.58	2464.58	71.12	0.83
1980-81	2086.10	992.92	1093.18	52.40	3888.21	1218.60	2669.61	68.66	0.76
1981-82	2527.02	1054.23	1472.79	58.28	4867.52	1319.63	3547.89	72.89	0.80

Note : A stands for agricultural sector.
N stands for non-agricultural sector.

Tabele 6.4: Growth of Potential Surplus in the A and N Sectors in Punjab (Fourth Approximation)

Years	*A Sector*				*N Sector*				*Ratio of (5) to (8)*
	Per capita income (Rs.)	*Per capita minimum consumption plus investment (Rs.)*	*Potential surplus (Rs.)*	*(4) as percentage of (2)*	*Per capita income (Rs.)*	*Per Capita minimum consumption plus investment (Rs.)*	*Potential surplus (Rs.)*	*(8) as percentage of (6)*	
1	2	3	4	5	6	7	8	9	10
1967-68	851.30	509.66	341.64	40.13	825.37	574.17	251.20	30.43	1.32
1968-69	915.76	508.04	407.72	44.52	907.24	572.61	334.63	36.88	1.21
1969-70	977.20	524.39	452.81	46.34	980.45	606.66	373.79	38.12	1.22
1970-71	1003.02	521.93	481.09	47.96	1101.57	612.79	488.78	44.37	1.08
1971-72	1043.98	547.95	496.03	47.51	1167.20	624.25	542.95	46.52	1.02
1972-73	1115.87	585.58	530.29	47.52	1289.74	697.51	592.23	45.92	1.03
1973-74	1474.02	739.53	734.49	49.83	1406.91	843.04	563.87	40.08	1.24
1974-75	1514.93	888.25	626.88	41.37	1565.97	1051.35	514.62	32.86	1.26
1975-76	1487.27	820.11	667.16	44.86	2202.38	1077.79	1124.59	51.06	0.88
1976-77	1742.65	833.99	908.66	52.14	2494.36	1074.73	1419.63	56.91	0.92
1977-78	1876.27	906.11	970.16	51.71	2827.16	1247.07	1580.09	55.89	0.92
1978-79	1921.65	912.07	1009.58	52.54	3059.59	1256.09	1803.50	58.94	0.89
1979-80	2086.52	1018.55	1067.97	51.18	3465.16	1442.73	2022.43	58.84	0.87
1980-81	2086.10	1161.68	924.42	44.31	3888.21	1714.73	2173.48	55.90	0.79
1981-82	2527.02	1258.67	1268.35	50.19	4867.52	1940.72	2926.80	60.13	0.83

Note : A stands for agricultural sector.
N stands for non-agricultural sector.

Table 6.5: Relative Potential Surplus of A and N Sectors in Punjab

(All Approximations)

Years	*First approximation*	*Second approximation*	*Third approximation*	*Fourth approximation*
1967-68	1.21	1.51	1.12	1.32
1968-69	1.12	1.31	1.06	1.21
1969-70	1.13	1.32	1.07	1.22
1970-71	1.01	1.13	0.98	1.08
1971-72	0.96	1.06	0.94	1.02
1972-73	0.97	1.08	0.95	1.03
1973-74	1.15	1.34	1.10	1.24
1974-75	1.16	1.41	1.08	1.26
1975-76	0.83	0.89	0.83	0.89
1976-77	0.87	0.92	0.86	0.92
1977-78	0.88	0.93	0.87	0.92
1978-79	0.85	0.89	0.84	0.89
1979-80	0.83	0.88	0.83	0.89
1980-81	0.75	0.78	0.76	0.79
1981-82	0.79	0.83	0.80	0.83

Note : A stands for agricultural sector.
N stands for non-agricultural sector.

Table 6.6: Index numbers of parity with the base year 1967-68 to 1969-70

Years	*Index numbers of prices received*	*Index numbers of prices paid*			*Index numbers of parity*
		domestic expen-diture	*cost of culti-vation*	*overall*	
1967-68	98.46	98.84	87.99	93.16	105.69
1968-69	100.89	100.01	102.94	101.54	99.36
1969-70	100.65	101.15	109.07	105.30	98.58
1970-71	100.60	106.75	117.24	112.24	89.63
1971-72	107.05	117.50	123.35	120.56	88.79
1972-73	122.22	132.02	136.04	134.13	91.12
1973-74	160.87	156.59	144.59	150.31	107.02
1974-75	175.41	189.22	154.00	170.78	102.71
1975-76	154.01	178.58	152.89	165.13	93.26
1976-77	166.68	220.89	161.66	189.88	87.78
1977-78	174.79	203.19	170.67	186.16	93.89
1978-79	190.00	201.19	178.04	189.07	100.49
1979-80	195.39	226.36	192.25	208.51	93.71
1980-81	258.06	270.67	229.92	249.34	103.50

Table 6.7: Index numbers of different commodities in Punjab (Base: 1967-68 to 1969-70=100)

Years	*Whole sale prices of 50 agri-cultural and ind-ustrial commodi-ties in Punjab*	*Whole sale prices of 21 agricu-ltural commodi-ties in Punjab*	*Harvest prices*			*Ratio of 4 to 2*	*Ratio of 5 to 2*	*Ratio of 6 to 2*	*Ratio of 4 to 3*	*Ratio of 5 to 3*	*Ratio of 6 to 3*
			Paddy	*Wheat*	*Cotton (American)*						
1	2	3	4	5	6	7	8	9	10	11	12
1967-68	99.95	95.96	89.16	95.78	91.68	0.89	0.96	0.92	0.92	0.96	0.92
1968-69	97.39	102.46	102.95	101.34	105.18	1.06	1.04	1.08	1.00	0.09	1.03
1969-70	102.66	101.58	107.91	102.87	103.14	1.05	1.00	1.00	1.06	1.01	1.02
1970-71	100.67	99.62	119.14	95.37	149.87	1.18	0.95	1.49	1.20	0.96	1.50
1971-72	101.33	101.53	149.00	97.46	129.84	1.47	0.96	1.28	1.47	0.96	1.28
1972-73	113.61	108.62	N.A.	94.92	109.47	—	0.84	0.96	—	0.87	1.01
1973-74	141.45	130.83	145.10	142.84	162.64	1.03	1.01	1.15	1.11	1.09	1.24
1974-75	181.53	167.12	157.26	134.54	185.56	0.87	0.74	1.02	0.94	0.81	1.11
1975-76	169.86	155.87	159.16	131.15	141.34	0.94	0.77	0.83	1.02	0.84	0.91
1976-77	161.26	147.26	149.31	137.37	244.35	0.93	0.85	1.52	1.01	0.93	1.66

1977-78	188.95	169.95	151.15	142.58	217.69	0.80	0.75	1.15	0.89	0.84	1.28
1978-79	184.54	160.47	156.78	145.84	169.09	0.85	0.79	0.92	0.98	0.91	1.05
1979-80	213.31	173.03	175.88	149.00	199.26	0.82	0.70	0.93	1.02	0.86	1.15
1980-81	259.77	221.74	192.63	166.50	225.01	0.74	0.64	0.87	0.87	0.75	1.01
1981-82	281.32	246.59	219.47	272.40	N.A.	0.78	0.97	—	0.89	1.10	—

Table 6.8: Index numbers of different commodities in Punjab (Base: 1967-68 to 1969-70 = 100)

Years	*Wholesale prices of 50 (agricultural + industrial) commodities in Punjab*	*Wholesale prices of 21 agricultural commodities*	*Harvest prices*				*Ratio of*							
			Barley	*Bajra*	*Maize*	*Gram*	*3 to 1*	*4 to 1*	*5 to 1*	*6 to 1*	*3 to 2*	*4 to 2*	*5 to 2*	*6 to 2*
	1	2	3	4	5	6	7	8	9	10	11	12	13	14
1967-68	99.95	95.96	99.12	88.79	98.20	81.08	0.99	0.89	0.98	0.81	1.03	0.93	1.10	0.84
1968-69	97.39	102.46	96.86	111.96	101.71	113.20	0.99	1.15	1.04	1.16	0.95	1.09	0.99	1.10
1969-70	102.66	101.58	104.00	99.23	100.07	105.73	1.01	0.97	0.99	1.03	1.02	0.98	0.99	1.04
1970-71	100.67	99.62	83.06	96.43	96.13	94.71	0.82	0.95	0.95	0.94	0.83	0.97	0.96	0.95
1971-72	101.33	101.53	114.65	93.28	98.48	94.71	1.13	0.92	0.97	0.93	1.13	0.92	0.97	0.93
1972-73	113.62	108.62	175.03	144.01	108.23	165.19	1.54	1.27	0.95	1.45	1.16	1.33	1.00	1.52
1973-74	141.45	130.83	199.23	151.80	136.14	229.27	1.41	1.07	0.96	1.62	1.52	1.16	1.04	1.75
1974-75	181.53	167.12	172.45	266.70	231.56	216.24	0.95	1.47	1.28	1.19	1.03	1.60	1.39	1.29
1975-76	169.86	155.87	109.27	137.97	137.12	125.11	0.64	0.81	0.84	0.74	0.79	0.89	0.88	0.82

1976-77	161.26	147.26	174.27	139.86	167.94	170.31	1.08	0.87	1.04	1.06	1.18	0.98	1.	1.16
1977-78	188.95	169.95	156.38	179.95	194.65	197.68	0.83	0.95	1.03	1.05	0.92	1.06	1.15	1.16
1978-79	184.54	160.47	145.67	144.12	187.63	207.94	0.79	0.78	1.02	1.13	0.91	0.90	1.17	1.30
1979-80	213.31	173.03	208.75	193.76	192.71	314.66	0.98	0.91	0.90	1.48	1.21	1.12	1.11	1.82
1980-81	259.77	221.74	219.64	196.24	233.87	388.68	0.85	0.76	0.90	1.50	0.90	0.89	1.05	1.75
1981-82	281.32	246.59	189.44	214.42	382.07	312.36	0.67	0.76	1.36	1.11	0.77	0.87	1.55	1.27

Table 6.9: Difference Between the Incomes at Current Prices and Constant Prices of Agricultural and Non-Agricultural Sectors 1971-72 to 1981-82

(Rs. in crores)

Years	*Agricultural sector*			*Non-Agricultural sector*		
	Current	*Constant*	*Difference*	*Current*	*Constant*	*Difference*
1	2	3	4	5	6	7
1971-72	880.44	858.22	22.22	597.32	572.72	24.60
1972-73	956.44	856.75	99.69	678.85	617.72	61.13
1973-74	1284.00	897.09	396.91	761.61	638.62	122.99
1974-75	1341.10	931.34	409.76	871.82	640.06	231.76
1975-76	1337.97	972.51	365.46	1260.96	799.06	461.90
1976-77	1593.10	1008.80	584.30	1468.65	876.95	591.70
1977-78	1742.97	1087.55	655.42	1711.77	956.27	755.56
1978-79	1813.91	1165.73	648.18	1904.93	1029.73	875.20
1979-80	2001.11	1138.79	862.43	2218.43	1068.27	1150.16
1980-81	2032.94	1124.53	908.41	2259.55	1161.37	1398.18
1981-82	2502.07	1294.44	1207.63	3294.57	1355.41	1939.16
			6150.41			7612.34

Table 6.10: Annual Production and Market Arrivals in Punjab (in '000 metric tonnes)

Years	*Wheat*		*Paddy*		*Maize*	
	Production	*Market arrivals*	*Production*	*Market arrivals*	*Production*	*Market arrivals*
1967-68	3335	1607 (48.2)	612	371 (60.6)	774	282 (36.4)
1968-69	4491	2295 (51.1)	705			
1969-70	4865	2722 (55.9)	802			
1970-71	5145	3121 (60.7)	1032	846 (82.0)	861	298 (34.6)
1971-72	5618	3414 (60.8)	1380	1255 (90.9)	857	338 (39.4)
1972-73	5368	2828 (52.7)	1432	1198 (83.7)	906	237 (26.2)
1973-74	5181	2171 (41.9)	1710	1465 (85.8)	764	122 (16.0)
1974-75	5286	2451 (46.4)	1768	1475 (83.4)	898	331 (36.9)
1975-76	5788	3063 (52.9)	1275	1836 (84.4)	846	195 (23.1)
1976-77	6392	3415 (53.4)	2664	2432 (91.3)	619	133 (21.5)
1977-78	6642	3317 (50.5)	3736	3435 (91.9)	678	105 (15.5)
1978-79	7439	4317 (58.0)	4612	4325 (93.8)	689	106 (15.4)
1979-80	7868	4392 (55.8)	4555	4294 (94.3)	677	61 (9.0)
1980-81	7674	3941 (51.3)	4850	4309 (89.4)	613	56 (9.1)
1981-82	8544	4896 (57.30)	5625	5166 (91.84)	625	37 (5.92)

Note: Figures in parenthesis show percentages to total production.

Source: Government of Punjab, Statistical Absract of Punjab: Various Issues.

Table 6.11: Percentage Distribution of Market Arrivals of Wheat and Rice

Crop	*Years*	*Percentage for the quarter*				*Number of Reporting Markets*
		April to June	*July to September*	*October to December*	*January to March*	
Wheat	1961-62	52.5	22.3	15.6	9.6	6
	1970-71	70.1	19.6	7.6	2.7	
	1979-80	92.1	5.7	1.2	1.0	
		October to December	*January to March*	*April to June*	*July to September*	
Rice	1961-62	71.6	26.6	1.8	-	
	1970-71	87.2	9.3	2.2	1.3	
	1978-79	96.5	3.2	0.2	0.1	

Source: A.S. Kahlon and D.S.Tyagi, *op.cit.*, pp. 422-24.

Table 6.12: Production and Procurement of Wheat and Rice in Punjab and India

Years	Wheat in Punjab			Procurement in India (in '000 MT)	Column 3 as percentage of column 5	Rice in Punjab			Procurement in India	Column 8 as percentage of column 10
	Production (in '000 MT)	Procurement in 000 MT)	Column 3 as percentage of column 2.			Production (in '000 MT)	Procurement (in 000 MT)	Column 8 as percentage of column 7		
1	2	3	4	5	6	7	8	9	10	11
1967-68	3335	570	17.09	779	73.17	415	—	—	2785	—
1968-69	4491	1351	30.08	2373	56.93	470	257	54.68	3373	7.62
1969-70	4865	1862	38.27	2417	77.04	535	370	69.16	3581	10.33
1970-71	5145	2400	46.65	3183	75.40	688	462	67.15	3043	15.18
1971-72	5618	2938	52.30	5008	58.67	920	771	83.80	3116	24.74
1972-73	5368	3171	59.07	5024	63.12	955	754	78.95	2706	27.86
1973-74	5181	2707	52.25	4531	59.74	1140	943	82.72	3887	24.26
1974-75	5286	1075	20.34	1955	54.99	1179	970	82.27	3795	25.56
1975-76	5788	2364	40.84	4049	58.38	1447	1201	83.00	6322	19.00
1976-77	6392	2942	46.03	6602	44.56	1776	1534	86.37	4431	34.63
1977-78	6642	3415	51.41	5165	66.12	2497	2190	87.71	4431	34.13
1978-79	7439	3204	43.07	5470	58.57	3090	2608	84.40	5552	46.97
1979-80	7868	4200	53.38	8000	52.50	3052	2688	88.07	5725	46.95
1980-81	7674	4277	55.73	5866	72.91	3233	2797	86.51	521	53.69
1981-82	8544	3766	44.08	6587	57.17	3743(P)	2822	75.39	6151	45.88

Source: G.K.Chadha, *The State and Rural Economic Transformation: The Case of Punjab, 1950-85*, (Sage Publications India, Pvt. Ltd. New Delhi, 1986).

Table 6.13: Production Cost, Procurement Prices and Net Returns from Wheat Cultivation from 1967-68 to 1981-82

(Rs/quintal)

Years	Production Cost A^*_2	Production Cost C**	Procurement Price (Rs.)	Difference in procurement price and cost of production in money terms (Rs.) (4–2)	Difference in procurement price and cost of production in money terms (Rs.) (4–3)	Rate of return over cost percentage $\frac{\text{col. 5}}{\text{col. 2}} \times 100$	Rate of return over cost percentage $\frac{\text{col. 6}}{\text{col. 3}} \times 100$	Difference in procurement price and cost of production (in real terms) base 1967-68*** (4–2)	
1	2	3	4	5	6	7	8	9	10
1967-68	30.37	50.02	71.00	40.63	20.98	133.78	41.94	40.63	20.98
1968-69	37.94	67.45	76.00	38.06	8.55	100.32	12.68	35.64	8.01
1969-70	35.03	62.69	76.00	40.97	13.31	116.96	21.23	38.70	12.57
1970-71	28.44	61.04	76.00	47.56	14.96	167.27	24.51	48.81	14.41
1971-72	31.37	59.71	76.00	44.63	16.29	142.27	27.28	42.18	18.40
1972-73	36.65	67.10	76.00	39.35	8.90	107.37	13.26	34.76	7.86
1973-74	41.08	74.34	105.00	63.92	30.66	155.60	41.24	46.88	22.49
1974-75	42.00	87.76	105.00	63.00	17.24	150.00	19.64	36.17	9.90
1975-76	50.91	99.45	105.00	54.09	5.55	106.27	5.58	33.30	3.42
1976-77	56.27	101.39	110.00	53.73	8.61	95.49	8.49	35.01	5.61
1977-78	62.65	108.57	112.50	49.85	3.93	79.57	3.62	28.14	2.22
1978-79	60.74	101.45	115.00	54.26	11.55	86.04	11.38	32.45	6.91
1979-80	62.28	102.76	117.00	54.77	14.24	87.86	13.86	30.34	7.90
1980-81	77.52	124.70	130.00	52.48	5.30	67.70	4.25	22.71	2.29
1981-82	75.19	118.77	142.00	66.81	23.23	88.85	19.56	26.00	9.04

* Cost 'A_2' covers paid-out expenses on material-inputs hired human labour bullock and machine labour expenses and rent paid for leased in land.

** Cost C includes both paid out as well as inputed and rising cost on account of family's own resources.

*** These figures have been worked out using the general price index of 21 agricultural commodities in Punjab (Appendix J)

Source: For figures upto 1974-75, Sidhu, *op.cit.*, 1979, pp. 75-81. For figures beyond 1974-75, Grewal and Rangi, "Wheat Cultivation: Economic of Punjab", *The Economic Times,* 26 August, 1982, p. 5, and Reports of the Commission for Agricultural Costs and Prices.

For consumer price index, Government of Punjab, Statistical Abstract of Punjab for various years.

Table 6.14: Composition of Tax Revenue in Punjab

Years	Share of taxes income	Share of union excise duty	Estate duty	Land revenue	State excise duty	Sales tax	Motor vehicles tax	Stamp duty & registe-ration fee	Passenger and goods tax	Enter-tainment tax	Electri-city duty	Other taxes	Total
1	2	3	4	5	6	7	8	9	10	11	12	13	14
1967-68	418.81	625.25	12.92	185.00	1515.05	1806.37	95.97	621.05	382.36	115.61	223.93	74.39	6076.80
	(6.89)	(10.29)	(0.21)	(3.04)	(24.93)	(29.73)	(1.58)	(10.22)	(6.29)	(1.90)	(3.68)	(1.22)	(100.00)
1968-69	466.65	799.00	14.59	186.98	2194.15	2485.41	123.63	683.05	451.56	139.35	244.01	114.35	7902.73
	(5.90)	(10.11)	(0.18)	(2.37)	(27.76)	(31.45)	(1.56)	(8.64)	(5.71)	(1.76)	(3.09)	(1.45)	(100.00)
1969-70	742.21	741.31	17.85	171.77	2252.14	3070.72	144.41	798.97	602.99	167.41	297.46	77.10	9084.34
	(8.17)	(8.16)	(10.19)	(1.89)	(24.79)	(33.80)	(1.59)	(8.80)	(6.64)	(1.84)	(3.27)	(0.85)	(100.00)
1970-71	904.95	900.89	18.24	168.69	2283.07	3728.09	174.11	930.70	734.60	203.36	306.88	70.49	10424.13
	(8.68)	(8.64)	(0.17)	(1.62)	(21.90)	(35.76)	(1.67)	(8.93)	(7.05)	(1.95)	(2.94)	(0.68)	(100.00)
1971-72	1159.42	1104.33	25.11	118.50	3139.63	4609.18	190.88	1000.79	826.38	248.52	311.02	63.98	11508.87
	(10.70)	(9.60)	(0.72)	(1.03)	(23.37)	(32.75)	(1.66)	(8.69)	(7.18)	(2.16)	(2.70)	(0.56)	(100.00)
1972-73	1231.78	1316.51	35.48	135.06	2690.51	3769.43	288.59	1138.15	912.08	262.77	382.35	90.36	13541.94
	(19.10)	(9.72)	(0.26)	(1.00)	(23.18)	(34.04)	(2.13)	(8.40)	(6.74)	(1.94)	(2.82)	(0.67)	(100.00)
1973-74	1330.70	1479.13	35.96	112.70	3462.70	5250.98	325.83	1263.59	1120.40	332.39	439.14	7.55	15160.13
	(8.78)	(9.76)	(0.24)	(0.74)	(22.84)	(34.64)	(2.14)	(8.33)	(7.39)	(2.19)	(2.90)	(0.05)	(100.00)
1974-75	1408.88	1454.14	29.83	183.24	3988.43	6334.82	560.65	1764.53	1361.71	476.12	479.58	12.13	18504.06
	(7.80)	(8.05)	(0.17)	(1.01)	(22.09)	(35.09)	(3.11)	(9.77)	(7.54)	(2.64)	(2.66)	(0.07)	(100.00)
1975-76	2018.79	1774.17	25.31	294.96	4549.87	7315.57	569.95	1847.90	1517.96	565.73	617.87	—	21098.08
	(9.57)	(8.41)	(0.12)	(1.40)	(21.57)	(34.67)	(2.70)	(8.76)	(7.19)	(2.68)	(2.93)	—	(100.00)

1976-77	1793.60	2127.00	33.22	229.91	4904.58	9612.41	635.93	1728.06	1682.95	610.27	800.00	6.31	24152.00
	(7.43)	(8.81)	(0.14)	(0.95)	(20.37)	(39.80)	(2.60)	(7.16)	(6.97)	(2.53)	(3.31)	(0.03)	(100.00)
1977-78	1857.00	2326.37	37.50	247.12	6230.09	10751.43	727.72	2150.77	1928.61	638.96	838.38	1.91	27732.04
	(6.70)	(8.40)	(0.13)	(0.89)	(22.47)	(38.77)	(2.62)	(7.76)	(6.95)	(2.30)	(3.02)	(0.01)	(100.00)
1978-79	1355.37	3164.39	48.48	261.50	6635.85	11930.85	912.63	2766.84	2115.19	788.71	1269.57	26.48	31275.86
	(4.33)	(10.12)	(0.16)	(0.84)	(21.22)	(38.15)	(2.92)	(8.85)	(6.76)	(2.52)	(4.06)	(0.08)	(100.00)
1979-80	2347.28	4955.34	33.26	264.58	8822.51	12979.15	1031.56	3018.08	2311.79	849.35	1622.46	5.54	38240.90
	(6.14)	(12.96)	(0.09)	(0.69)	(23.07)	(33.94)	(2.70)	(7.89)	(6.05)	(2.22)	(4.24)	(0.01)	(100.00)
1980-81	2724.95	5426.96	67.46	241.77	9312.44	15593.08	1078.12	3582.95	2617.87	942.00	1502.82	15.00	43105.00
	(6.32)	(12.59)	(0.16)	(0.56)	(21.60)	(36.17)	(2.50)	(8.31)	(6.07)	(2.18)	(3.49)	(0.03)	(100.00)
1981-82	2881.82	6282.00	52.07	319.07	11603.38	19181.94	1626.80	4675.52	3255.21	1015.46	1536.57	12.17	52442.00
	(5.49)	(11.98)	(0.10)	(0.61)	(22.13)	(36.58)	(3.10)	(8.91)	(6.21)	(1.94)	(2.93)	(0.02)	(100.00)
Compound Growth rate (per cent)	12.93	17.66	10.00	4.94	14.41	17.17	21.89	14.77	15.59	17.55	16.74	–19.24	15.76
Buoyancy	1.98*	1.35*	0.77*	0.42*	1.12	1.31*	1.63*	1.14*	1.22*	1.33*	1.20*	–1.77*	1.21*
co-efficient	(7.19)	(19.63)	(7.14)	(2.81)	(25.09)	(29.95)	(24.61)	(19.77)	(19.66)	(22.44)	(27.66)	(12.13)	(31.86)

* denotes significant at 5 per cent level of significance.
Figures in parenthesis are t̄-values.

Table 6.15: Per Capita Tax Burden and Per Capita Income of A Sector and N Sector in Punjab

Years	*A Sector*			*N Sector*					
	Per capita tax burden (Rupees)	*Per capita income (Rupees)*	*(2) as percentage of (3)*	*Per capita tax buden (Rupees)*	*Per capta income (Rupees)*	*(5) as Percentage of (6)*	*Ratio of (2) to (5)*	*Ratio of (3) to (6)*	*Ratio of (4) to (7)*
1	2	3	4	5	6	7	8	9	10
1967-68	36.73	851.30	4.31	39.26	825.37	4.76	0.94	1.03	0.91
1968-69	47.34	915.76	5.17	52.01	907.24	5.73	0.91	1.01	0.90
1969-70	54.39	977.20	5.57	57.21	980.45	5.84	0.95	1.00	0.95
1970-71	60.62	1003.02	6.04	63.67	1101.57	5.78	0.95	0.91	1.04
1971-72	63.83	1043.98	6.11	67.70	1167.20	5.80	0.94	0.89	1.05
1972-73	69.85	1115.87	6.26	86.43	1289.74	6.70	0.81	0.87	0.93
1973-74	75.16	1474.02	5.10	98.13	1406.91	6.97	0.77	1.05	0.73
1974-75	85.07	1514.93	5.62	123.43	1565.97	7.88	0.69	0.97	0.71
1975-76	99.19	1487.27	6.67	131.09	2202.38	5.95	0.76	0.68	1.12
1976-77	119.45	1742.65	6.85	150.59	2494.36	6.04	0.79	0.70	1.13
1977-78	135.81	1876.27	7.24	165.00	2827.16	5.84	0.82	0.66	1.24
1978-79	149.58	1921.65	7.72	186.31	3059.59	6.09	0.80	0.63	1.28
1979-80	177.62	2086.52	8.51	199.40	3465.16	5.75	0.89	0.60	1.48
1980-81	189.37	2086.10	9.08	233.70	3888.21	6.01	0.81	0.54	1.51
1981-82	229.62	2527.02	9.09	285.91	4867.52	5.87	0.80	0.52	1.55

Note : A stands for agricultural sector.
N stands for non-agricultural sector.

Table 6.16: Per Capita Tax Burden on Different Expenditure Groups in A Sector (Rupees)

Expenditure groups with per capita monthly consumption expenditure (Rupees)	*State excise duty*	*Sales tax*	*Motor vehicles tax*	*Stamp duty and registration fee*	*Electricity duty*	*Entertainment tax*	*Passenger tax*	*Goods tax*	*Total*
1	2	3	4	5	6	7	8	9	10
Less than 40	—	6.06	0.91	9.26	1.55	—	2.48	0.53	20.79
40-60	—	35.95	2.56	9.26	2.22	—	7.57	0.70	58.26
60-70	2.60	40.22	3.43	9.26	2.87	—	10.21	0.87	69.46
70-80	5.52	46.82	2.08	9.26	3.50	—	5.85	1.03	74.06
80-100	18.28	50.70	3.14	9.26	5.22	0.62	8.71	1.15	97.07
100-150	83.55	54.10	7.56	9.26	4.52	1.06	22.42	1.62	184.09
150-200	188.17	95.73	9.75	9.26	7.76	1.68	23.04	2.24	337.63
200 and above	211.72	201.23	8.34	9.26	14.04	5.94	30.51	3.25	484.29
All groups	47.20	54.72	4.69	9.26	4.40	0.72	13.54	1.28	135.81

Note : A stands for agricultural sector.

Table 6.17: Per Capita Tax Burden on Different Expenditure Groups in N Sector

(Rupees)

Expenditure groups with per capita monthly consumption expenditure (Rupees)	*State excise duty*	*Sales tax*	*Motor vehicles tax*	*Stamp duty and registration fee*	*Electricity duty*	*Entertainment tax*	*Passenger tax*	*Goods tax*	*Total*
1	2	3	4	5	6	7	8	9	10
Less than 40	—	18.06	0.16	21.31	3.93	—	—	0.46	43.92
40-60	—	39.11	0.70	21.31	3.90	3.22	0.95	0.70	69.89
60-70	—	46.13	0.30	21.31	4.04	4.21	—	0.87	76.86
70-80	4.03	59.37	0.47	21.31	4.65	7.90	0.32	0.93	98.98
80-100	38.46	56.45	4.74	21.31	5.14	11.50	8.82	1.08	147.60
100-150	48.33	92.78	5.05	21.31	9.87	10.35	8.58	1.57	197.84
150-200	69.19	157.40	8.56	21.31	11.17	14.02	12.87	2.04	296.56
200 and above	100.75	330.07	34.71	21.31	19.66	30.68	54.98	3.71	595.87
All groups	30.48	82.72	4.82	21.31	7.08	9.44	7.83	1.29	164.97

Note : N stands for non-agricultural sector.

Table 6.18 : Per Capita Tax Burden on Different Expenditure Groups in Punjab

(Overall Rupees)

Expenditure groups with per capita monthly consumption expenditure (Rupees)	*State excise duty*	*Sales tax*	*Motor vehicles tax*	*Stamp duty and registration fee*	*Electricity duty*	*Entertainment tax*	*Passenger tax*	*Goods tax*	*Total*
1	2	3	4	5	6	7	8	9	10
Less than 40	—	10.02	0.66	14.02	2.33	—	1.66	0.51	29.30
40-60	—	37.14	1.86	14.02	2.85	1.21	5.08	0.70	62.86
60-70	1.61	42.46	2.24	14.02	3.31	1.61	6.34	0.87	72.45
70-80	4.93	51.78	1.45	14.02	3.95	3.12	3.66	0.99	83.90
80-100	26.77	53.11	3.81	14.02	5.19	5.17	8.76	1.13	117.96
100-150	70.04	68.94	6.60	14.02	6.57	4.62	17.11	1.60	189.50
150-200	138.34	121.56	9.25	14.02	9.19	6.85	18.78	2.16	320.15
200 and above	159.38	262.00	20.78	14.02	16.69	17.61	42.05	3.47	536.00
All groups	40.60	65.77	0.74	14.02	5.46	4.16	11.28	1.28	147.31

Table 6.19: Share of Different Expenditure Groups in Total Annual Consumption Expenditure and their Respective Share in State Taxes and Population in A sector

Expenditure groups with per capita monthly consumption expenditure (Rs.)	*Population of households*		*Consumption expenditure of households*		*State taxes*		*Consumption expenditure less state taxes*	
	Percentage share	*Cumulative percentage share*	*Percenage share*	*Cumulative percentage share*	*Percentage share*	*Cumulative percentage share*	*Percentage share*	*Cumulative percentage share*
1	2	3	4	5	6	7	8	9
Less than 40	2.78	2.78	1.16	1.16	0.43	0.43	1.26	1.26
40-60	17.90	20.68	9.81	10.97	7.68	8.11	10.10	11.36
60-70	13.51	34.19	9.22	20.19	6.91	15.02	9.54	20.90
70-80	11.68	45.87	9.37	29.56	6.37	21.39	9.78	30.68
80-100	17.73	63.60	16.00	45.56	12.67	34.06	14.46	47.14
100-150	25.23	88.83	31.95	70.51	34.20	68.26	31.64	78.78
150-200	7.49	96.32	13.14	90.65	18.62	86.88	12.38	9.16
200 amd above	3.68	100.00	9.35	100.00	13.12	100.00	8.84	100.00
Concentration ratio				0.2378		0.3702		0.2199

Note: A stands for agricultural sector.

Table 6.20: Share of Different Expenditure Groups in Total Annual Consumption Expenditure and their Respective Share of State Taxes and Population in N Sector

Expenditure groups with per capita monthly consumption expenditure (Rs.)	*Population of households*		*Consumption expenditure of households*		*Indesed taxes*		*Consumption expenditure less state taxes*	
	Percentage share	*Cumulative percentage share*	*Percenage share*	*Cumulative percentage share*	*Percentage share*	*Cumulative percentage share*	*Percentage share*	*Cumulative percentage share*
1	2	3	4	5	6	7	8	9
Less than 40	2.10	2.10	0.75	0.75	0.56	0.56	0.78	0.78
40-60	16.50	18.60	9.94	9.69	6.99	7.55	9.25	10.03
60-70	12.66	31.26	8.53	18.22	5.90	13.45	8.94	18.97
70-80	11.73	42.99	8.42	26.64	7.04	20.49	8.63	27.60
80-100	19.60	62.59	16.47	43.11	17.54	38.03	16.30	43.90
100-150	24.09	86.68	29.31	72.42	28.89	66.92	29.38	73.28
150-200	8.28	94.96	13.09	85.51	14.88	81.80	12.81	86.09
200 and above	5.04	100.00	14.49	100.00	18.20	100.00	13.91	100.00
Concentration ratio				0.2504		0.3378		0.3138

Note : N stands for non-agricultural sector.

Table 6.21: Share of Different Expenditure Groups in Total Annual Consumption Expenditure and their Respective Share of Taxes and Population in Punjab

Expenditure groups with per capita monthly consumption expenditure (Rs.)	*Population of households*		*Consumption expenditure of households*		*State taxes*		*Consumption expenditure less state taxes*	
	Percentage share	*Cumulative percentage share*	*Percenage share*	*Cumulative percentage share*	*Percentage share*	*Cumulative percentage share*	*Percentage share*	*Cumulative percentage share*
1	2	3	4	5	6	7	8	9
Less than 40	2.51	2.51	0.99	0.99	0.50	0.50	1.06	1.06
40-60	17.35	19.86	9.45	10.44	7.40	7.50	9.75	10.81
60-70	13.17	33.03	8.94	19.38	6.48	14.36	9.29	20.10
70-80	11.70	44.73	8.97	28.35	6.66	21.04	9.30	29.40
80-100	18.47	63.20	16.19	44.54	14.79	35.83	16.40	45.80
100-150	24.78	87.98	30.85	13.12	31.88	67.71	38.70	76.50
150-200	7.80	95.78	13.12	88.51	16.95	84.66	12.56	89.06
200 and above	4.22	100.00	11.49	100.00	15.34	100.00	10.94	100.00
Concentration ratio				0.2456		0.3574		0.2296

Table 6.22: Receipts and expenditure on revenue account

(Lakh Rupees)

Years	*Receipts*	*Expenditure*	*Surplus(+) or Deficit(-)*
1967-68	10545.42	9683.79	861.63
1968-69	11947.22	10713.52	1233.70
1969-70	13881.24	11735.05	2146.19
1970-71	16878.07	13296.10	3581.97
1971-72	17420.46	14261.09	3159.37
1972-73	21537.27	18919.78	2617.49
1973-74	23231.97	22469.59	762.38
1974-75	25001.56	22015.40	2986.16
1975-76	30440.51	27858.81	2581.70
1976-77	37641.07	31621.05	6020.02
1977-78	40611.57	34281.58	6329.99
1978-79	48097.80	38656.60	9441.20
1979-80	52744.52	44195.46	8549.06
1980-81	56766.00	54952.80	1813.20
1981-82	68261.40	61998.21	6263.19

Source: Economic and Statistical Organisation, Government of Punjab, *Statistical Abstract of Public Finance in Punjab*: *Various Issues.*

Table 6.23: Pattern of Development Expenditure in Punjab

(Lakh Rupees)

Years	Exp. on education art and culture	Medical and public health and family welfare	Transport and communication	Agricultrue and allied	Industry and minerals	Cooperation	Others	Total development and social service expenditure
1	2	3	4	5	6	7	8	9
1967-68	2115.15	599.06	444.67	1486.71	205.83	88.07	827.95	5767.44
	(36.67)	(10.39)	(7.71)	(25.79)	(3.57)	(1.53)	(14.36)	(100.00)
1968-69	2529.45	726.77	490.60	1633.17	199.20	112.87	1105.86	6797.72
	(37.21)	(10.69)	(7.22)	(24.03)	(2.93)	(1.66)	(16.26)	(100.00)
1969-70	2774.94	845.10	590.93	1682.84	236.78	117.48	1555.21	7803.28
	(35.56)	(10.83)	(7.57)	(21.57)	(3.03)	(1.50)	(19.93)	(100.00)
1970-71	3017.27	985.92	671.38	2151.97	214.92	126.00	1712.98	8881.44
	(33.97)	(11.10)	(6.57)	(24.33)	(2.42)	(1.42)	(19.29)	(100.00)
1971-72	3153.28	1136.56	1072.07	2471.22	160.80	156.19	1829.96	9980.08
	(31.60)	(11.39)	(10.74)	(24.76)	(1.61)	(1.57)	(18.34)	(100.00)
1972-73	3976.20	1591.55	2577.58	1728.80	213.70	220.38	3415.52	13723.73
	(28.97)	(11.60)	(18.78)	(12.60)	(1.56)	(1.61)	(24.89)	(100.00)
1973-74	4746.14	1994.68	3112.84	1946.48	251.92	145.98	4562.64	16760.68
	(28.32)	(11.90)	(18.57)	(11.61)	(1.50)	(0.87)	(27.22)	(100.00)
1974-75	5467.17	1960.68	3072.70	1836.90	287.61	187.79	2684.16	15497.00
	(35.28)	(12.65)	(19.83)	(11.85)	(1.86)	(0.21)	(17.32)	(100.00)

1975-76	6481.86	2863.04	3390.20	3467.66	355.85	231.50	3287.40	20077.51
	(32.28)	(14.26)	(16.88)	(17.27)	(1.77)	(1.15)	(16.37)	(100.00)
1976-77	7044.36	2763.20	3894.84	3280.20	406.09	274.21	5129.57	22792.47
	(30.90)	(12.12)	(17.90)	(14.39)	(1.78)	(1.20)	(22.51)	(100.00)
1977-78	7823.01	3212.02	4460.17	4073.03	317.48	419.76	4484.40	24789.87
	(31.55)	(12.96)	(17.99)	(16.43)	(1.28)	(1.69)	(18.09)	(100.00)
1978-79	8938.90	3639.70	4978.22	3407.38	363.87	525.69	6507.53	28361.20
	(31.25)	(12.83)	(17.55)	(12.01)	(1.28)			(100.00)
1979-80	10126.88	4125.08	5841.43	4744.73	440.49	578.96	6786.87	32644.44
	(31.02)	(12.64)	(17.89)	(14.53)	(1.35)	(1.77)	(20.79)	(100.00)
1980-81	13767.07	4890.68	6489.20	5441.63	494.69	535.16	7905.79	39524.29
	(34.84)	(12.37)	(16.42)	(13.77)	(1.25)	(1.35)	(20.00)	(100.00)
1981-82	14421.83	5646.52	7450.22	6075.87	562.11	436.33	6551.28	41144.16
	(35.05)	(13.72)	(18.11)	(14.77)	(1.37)	(1.06)	(15.92)	(100.00)
Growth rate(percent)	14.78	17.38	23.85	10.30	7.93	14.57	16.25	15.26
Buoyancy co-efficient	1.12*	1.30*	1.72*	0.81*	0.64	1.10*	1.21*	1.15*
	(37.09)	(25.81)	(15.86)	(8.71)	(7.80)	(13.07)	(12.72)	(21.06)

*denotes significant at 5 per cent level.

Figures in Parenthesis are t-values.

The classification of developmental expenditure was changed in 1972-73. Therefore, the data for the preceding years were regrouped under the above sub-headings. Agriculture includes veterinary, forests, community development and irrigation. Others include civil works, multipurpose river valley schemes and miscellaneous. The fall in the expenditure figures for agriculture after 1972-73 is perhaps due to change in the classification.

Table 6.24: Per capita benefits from different items of expenditure in A and N sectors

(Rupees)

	Education			*Medican and public health services*			*Transport*			*Agricultural development* expenditure	*Industrial development expenditure*		*Cooperation*			*Other types*		
Years	A	N	O	A	N	O	A	N	O	A	N	O	A	N	O	A	N	O
1	2	3	4	5	6	7	8	9	10	11	12	13	14	15	16	17	18	19
1967-68	14.78	20.53	16.88	4.76	4.82	4.78	4.20	2.43	3.55	18.72	4.49	13.51	1.00	0.19	0.70	6.61	6.61	6.61
1968-69	17.43	23.85	19.80	5.66	5.74	5.69	4.55	2.63	3.84	20.25	4.23	14.34	1.26	0.24	0.88	8.65	8.65	8.65
1969-70	18.63	25.80	21.30	6.45	6.54	6.49	5.38	3.11	4.53	20.56	4.89	14.73	1.29	0.24	0.90	11.94	11.94	11.94
1970-71	21.19	25.23	22.71	7.38	7.48	7.42	6.00	3.47	5.05	25.90	4.32	17.91	1.36	0.25	0.95	12.89	12.89	12.89
1971-72	20.64	28.60	23.27	8.34	8.46	8.39	9.41	5.44	7.91	29.30	3.14	19.42	1.67	0.30	1.15	13.50	13.50	13.50
1972-73	24.86	35.06	28.74	11.44	11.60	11.50	22.19	12.83	18.63	20.17	4.06	14.04	2.31	0.42	1.59	24.69	24.69	24.69
1973-74	33.70	33.45	33.60	15.05	14.24	14.12	26.29	15.20	22.04	22.34	4.65	15.56	1.51	0.27	1.03	32.30	32.30	32.30
1974-75	38.95	26.28	37.91	13.53	13.71	13.60	25.46	14.71	21.31	20.75	5.17	14.73	1.15	0.34	1.30	18.61	18.61	18.61
1975-76	46.75	39.76	44.03	19.35	19.61	19.45	27.55	15.92	23.63	38.55	6.21	25.97	2.32	0.40	1.57	22.33	22.33	22.33
1976-77	52.48	38.15	46.87	18.29	18.54	18.38	31.04	17.95	25.91	35.88	6.90	24.53	2.70	0.47	1.82	34.13	34.13	34.13
1977-78	57.36	41.20	50.98	20.82	21.10	20.93	34.87	20.16	29.67	43.84	5.24	28.61	4.07	0.69	2.74	29.22	29.22	29.22
1978-79	64.50	45.78	57.06	23.11	23.42	23.23	38.18	22.67	31.78	36.16	5.84	24.67	5.01	0.84	3.35	41.54	41.54	41.54
1979-80	71.91	50.44	63.32	25.65	26.00	25.79	43.95	25.40	36.52	49.47	6.88	32.42	5.43	0.90	3.62	42.43	42.43	42.43
1980-81	97.48	64.83	84.32	29.79	30.19	29.95	47.89	27.68	39.74	55.84	7.51	36.36	4.94	0.81	3.28	48.41	48.41	48.41
1981-82	100.68	65.80	86.15	33.69	34.14	33.87	53.94	31.17	44.69	61.36	8.30	39.82	3.97	0.64	2.62	39.30	39.30	39.30

Compound growth rate (per cent)	15.33	7.91	12.45	15.00	15.00	15.00	21.51	21.50	21.34	8.56	4.96	7.82	12.78	11.46	12.28	13.89	13.89	13.89
Buoyancy Coefficient	1.81*	0.59*	1.15*	1.77*	1.06*	1.36*	2.49*	1.44*	1.86*	1.01*	0.39*	0.75*	1.45*	0.83*	1.12*	1.64*	0.45*	1.24*
	(31.19)	(9.17)	(31.75)	(24.81)	(17.63)	(22.88)	(19.73)	(11.85)	(14.96)	(6.57)	(4.05)	(7.28)	(9.16)	(10.61)	(11.62)	(12.74)	(2.29)	(10.34)

Note: *denotes significant at 5 per cent level.
Figures in parenthesis are t-values.
A stands for agricultural sector
N stands for non-agricultural sector
O stands for overall Punjab.

Table 6.25: Per Capita Expenditure Benefits—Absolute as well as in Relation to Per Capita Income

(Lakh Rupees)

Years	*Per capita expenditure benefits (In absolute terms) (Rupees)*				*Per capita expenditure benefits in relation to per capita income (Per cent)*			
	A sector	*N sector*	*Overall*	*Ratio of A to N*	*A sector*	*N sector*	*Overall*	*Ratio of A to N*
1	2	3	4	5	6	7	8	9
1967-68	50.07	39.07	46.03	1.28	5.88	4.73	5.47	1.24
1968-69	57.80	45.34	53.20	1.27	6.31	5.00	5.83	1.26
1969-70	64.25	52.52	59.89	1.22	6.57	5.36	6.12	1.23
1970-71	74.72	53.64	66.83	1.39	7.45	4.87	6.43	1.53
1971-72	82.26	59.44	73.64	1.38	7.88	5.09	6.75	1.55
1972-73	105.66	88.66	99.19	1.19	9.47	6.87	8.39	1.38
1973-74	130.19	100.11	118.65	1.30	8.83	7.11	8.19	1.24
1974-75	119.20	88.82	107.46	1.34	7.87	5.67	7.00	1.39
1975-76	156.85	104.23	136.38	1.50	10.55	4.73	7.72	2.23
1976-77	174.52	116.14	151.64	1.50	10.01	4.66	7.44	2.15
1977-78	190.18	117.61	161.55	1.62	10.14	4.16	7.17	2.44

1978-79	208.44	139.49	181.03	1.49	10.85	4.56	7.62	2.38
1979-80	238.84	152.05	204.10	1.57	11.45	4.39	7.74	2.61
1980-81	284.35	179.43	242.06	1.58	13.63	4.61	8.61	2.96
1981-82	292.94	179.35	246.81	1.63	11.59	3.68	7.10	3.15

Note: A stands for agricultural sector
N stands for non-agricultural sector

Table 6.26: Per Capita Benefits from Different Items of Development Expenditure for Different Expenditure Groups in Agricultural Sector

(Rupees)

Expenditure groups with per capita monthly consumption expenditure (Rupees)	*Education*	*Medical and public health*	*Transport*	*Cooperation*	*Other development expenditure*	*Total development expenditure**
1	2	3	4	5	6	7
Less than 40	18.02	4.04	6.40	4.07	29.22	61.75
40-60	19.88	8.84	19.50	4.07	29.22	81.51
60-70	35.14	15.14	16.30	4.07	29.22	99.87
70-80	48.17	21.10	25.08	4.07	29.22	127.64
800-100	62.13	23.83	22.44	4.07	29.22	141.69
100-150	73.46	25.17	57.76	4.07	29.22	189.68
150-200	101.89	33.18	62.30	4.07	29.22	230.66
200 and above	156.06	42.31	77.55	4.07	29.22	309.21
All groups	57.36	20.82	34.87	4.07	29.22	146.34

*Excluding benefits from agricultural development expenditure.

Table 6.27: Per Capita Benefits from Different Items of Development Expenditure for Different Expenditure Groups in Non-agricultural Sector

(Rs. in crores)

Expenditure groups with per capita monthly consumption expenditure (Rupees)	*Education*	*Medical and public health*	*Transport*	*Cooperation*	*Other development expenditure*	*Total development expenditure**	*Ratio of A to N sectors expenditure*
1	2	3	4	5	6	7	8
Less than 40	8.61	3.92	—	0.69	29.22	42.44	1.45
40-60	16.53	6.73	2.46	0.69	29.22	55.63	1.47
60-70	25.88	15.09	3.52	0.69	29.22	74.40	1.34
70-80	34.99	22.18	9.82	0.69	29.22	96.90	1.32
80-100	46.12	25.11	18.71	0.69	29.22	119.85	1.18
100-150	50.64	22.13	32.10	0.69	29.22	134.78	1.41
150-200	67.18	35.10	43.17	0.69	29.22	175.36	1.32
200 and above	82.59	44.43	63.17	0.69	29.22	220.10	1.40
All groups	41.20	21.10	20.16	0.69	29.22	112.43	1.30

*excluding benefits from industrial development expenditure.

Table 6.28: Per Capita Benefits from Different Items of Development Expenditure for Different Expenditure Groups in Punjab.

Rupees

Expenditure groups with monthly per capita consumption expenditure (Rupees)	*Education*	*Medical and public health*	*Transport*	*Cooperation*	*Other development expenditure*	*Total development expenditure**
1	2	3	4	5	6	7
Less than 40	14.92	4.00	4.29	2.96	29.22	55.38
40-60	18.62	8.05	13.10	2.80	29.22	71.80
60-70	31.63	15.12	11.45	2.79	29.22	90.21
70-80	42.96	21.53	19.04	2.73	29.22	115.48
80-100	55.43	24.37	20.88	2.65	29.22	132.54
100-150	64.71	24.00	47.92	2.77	29.22	168.62
150-200	87.35	33.98	54.29	2.65	29.22	207.50
200 and above	121.41	43.31	70.77	2.48	29.22	267.18
All groups	50.98	20.93	29.07	2.74	29.22	132.96

*Excluding benefits from agricultural and industrial development expenditure.

Table 6.29: Distribution of Per Capita Benefits in Relation to Per Capita Expenditure for Different Expenditure Groups in Agricultural Sector

(Per cent)

Expenditure groups with per capita consumption expenditure (Rupees)	*Education*	*Medical and public helath*	*Transport*	*Cooperation*	*Other development expenditure*	*Total development expenditure**
1	2	3	4	5	6	7
Less than 40	3.84	0.86	1.36	0.87	6.23	13.17
40-60	3.23	1.44	3.17	0.66	4.75	13.25
60-70	4.58	1.98	2.13	0.53	3.81	13.03
70-80	5.33	2.34	2.79	0.45	3.25	14.18
80-100	6.13	2.35	2.21	0.40	2.88	13.99
100-150	5.17	1.77	4.06	0.29	2.06	13.34
150-200	5.18	1.69	3.16	0.21	1.48	11.72
200 and above	5.47	1.48	2.72	0.14	1.02	10.84
All groups	5.11	1.85	3.11	0.36	2.60	13.04

* Excluding benefits from agricultural development expenditure.

Table 6.30: Distribution of Per Capita Benefits in Relation to Per Capita Expenditure for Different Expenditure Groups in Non-agricultural Sector

(Percent)

Expenditure groups with monthly per-capita consumption expenditure (Rupees)	*Education*	*Medical and public helath*	*Transport*	*Cooperation*	*Other development expenditure*	*Total development expenditure**
1	2	3	4	5	6	7
Less than 40	1.96	0.89	—	0.16	6.66	9.68
40-60	2.48	1.01	0.37	0.10	4.38	8.34
60-70	3.12	1.82	0.42	0.08	3.52	8.97
70-80	3.96	2.51	1.11	0.08	3.31	10.97
80-100	4.46	2.43	1.81	0.07	2.82	11.59
100-150	3.38	1.48	2.14	0.05	1.95	9.00
150-200	3.45	1.80	2.22	0.04	1.50	9.01
200 and above	2.33	1.26	1.78	0.02	0.83	6.22
All groups	3.35	1.71	1.64	0.06	2.37	9.13

* Excluding benefits from industrial development expenditure.

Table 6.31: Population, Total Consumption Expenditure and Expenditure Benefits* for Different Expenditure Groups in Agricultural Sector

Expenditure groups with per capita monthly consumption expenditure (Rupees)	Population		Consumption expenditure		Expenditure benefits		Consumption expenditure + expenditure benefits	
	Percentage share	Cumulative percentage share	Percenage share	Cumulative percentage share	Percentage share	Cumulative percentage share	Percentage share	Comulative percentage share
1	2	3	4	5	6	7	8	9
Less than 40	2.78	2.78	1.16	1.16	1.17	1.17	1.17	1.17
40-60	17.90	20.68	9.81	10.97	9.97	11.14	9.91	11.08
60-70	13.51	34.19	9.22	20.19	9.22	20.36	9.22	20.30
70-80	11.68	45.87	9.37	29.56	10.19	30.55	9.87	30.17
80-100	17.73	63.60	16.00	45.56	17.17	47.72	16.71	79.29
100-150	25.23	88.83	31.95	77.51	32.70	80.42	32.41	79.29
150-200	7.49	96.32	13.14	90.65	11.80	92.22	12.22	91.61
200 and above	3.68	100.00	9.35	100.00	7.78	100.00	8.39	100.00
Concentration ratio	—	—	—	0.2378	—	0.2135	—	0.2230

* Excluding benefits from agricultural development expenditure.

Table 6.32: Population, Total Consumption Expenditure and Expenditure Benefits* for Different Expenditure Groups in Non-Agricultural Sector

Expenditure groups with per capita monthly consumption expenditure (Rs.)	*Population*		*Consumption expenditure*		*Expenditure benefits*		*Consumption expenditure + expenditure benefits*	
	Percentage share	*Cumulative percentage share*	*Percentage share*	*Cumulative percentage share*	*Percentage share*	*Cumulative percentage share*	*Percentage share*	*Cumulative percentage share*
1	2	3	4	5	6	7	8	9
Less than 40	2.10	2.10	0.75	0.75	0.79	0.79	0.77	0.77
40-60	16.50	18.60	8.94	9.69	8.16	8.95	8.54	9.31
60-70	12.66	31.26	8.53	18.22	8.38	17.33	8.45	17.76
70-80	11.73	42.99	8.42	26.64	10.11	27.44	9.30	27.06
80-100	19.60	62.59	16.47	43.11	20.89	48.33	18.78	45.84
100-150	24.09	86.68	29.31	72.42	28.88	77.21	29.09	74.93
150-200	8.28	94.96	13.09	85.51	12.91	90.12	13.00	87.93
200 and above	5.04	100.00	14.49	100.00	9.88	100.00	12.07	100.00
Concentration ratio	—	—	—	0.2504	—	0.2127	—	0.2330

* Excluding benefits from industrial development expenditure.

Table 6.33: Population, Total Consumption Expenditure and Expenditure Benefits* for Different Expenditure Groups in Punjab

Expenditure groups with per capita monthly consumption expenditure (Rs.)	*Population*		*Consumption expenditure*		*Expenditure benefits*		*Consumption expenditure + expenditure benefits*	
	Percentage share	*Cumulative percentage share*	*Percenage share*	*Cumulative percentage share*	*Percentage share*	*Cumulative percentage share*	*Percentage share*	*Cumulative percentage share*
1	2	3	4	5	6	7	8	9
Less than 40	2.57	2.51	0.99	0.99	1.05	1.05	1.02	1.02
40-60	17.35	19.86	9.45	10.44	9.37	10.42	9.40	10.42
60-70	13.17	33.03	8.94	19.38	8.94	19.36	8.94	19.36
70-80	11.70	44.73	8.97	28.35	10.16	29.52	9.66	29.02
80-100	18.47	63.20	16.19	44.54	18.41	47.93	17.48	46.50
100-150	24.78	87.98	30.85	75.39	31.43	79.36	31.18	77.68
150-200	7.80	95.78	13.12	88.51	12.18	91.54	12.57	90.25
200 and above	4.22	100.00	11.49	100.00	8.46	100.00	9.75	100.00
Concertration ratio								

* Excluding benefits from agricultural and industrial development.

Table 6.34: Per Capita Benefits (including Agricultural and Non-Agricultural Development Expenditure Benefits) for Different Expenditure Groups

(Rupees)

Expenditure groups with per capita monthly consumption expenditure (Rupees)	*A Sector*	*N Sector*	*Overall Punjab*	*Ratio of A to N sectors' benefits*
1	2	3	4	5
Less than 40	98.81	43.46	80.55	2.27
40-60	124.03	58.05	99.27	2.14
60-70	141.54	77.13	117.12	1.84
70-80	177.30	100.09	146.76	1.77
80-100	188.21	123.90	161.28	1.52
100-150	228.85	141.93	195.51	1.61
150-200	275.15	183.31	236.69	1.50
200 and above	372.00	238.53	309.05	1.56
All groups	190.19	117.67	161.57	1.62

Note : A stands for agricultural sector.
N stands for non-agricultural sector.

Table 6.35: Per Capita Benefits (including Agricultural and Non-Agricultural Development Expenditure Benefits) in relation to per capita expenditure for Different Expenditure Groups

(Per cent)

Expenditure group with per capita monthly consumption expenditure (Rupees)	*A Sector*	*N Sector*	*Overall Punjab*	*Ratio of A to N sectors' benefits*
1	2	3	4	5
Less than 40	21.08	9.91	17.55	2.13
40-60	20.16	8.70	15.64	2.32
60-70	18.47	9.30	14.82	1.99
70-80	19.70	11.33	16.43	1.74
80-100	18.58	11.98	15.78	1.55
100-150	16.10	9.48	13.48	1.70
150-200	13.98	9.42	12.08	1.48
200 and above	13.04	6.74	9.73	1.93
All groups	16.94	9.56	13.86	1.77

Note : A stands for agricultural sector.
N stands for non-agricultural sector.

Table 6.36: Percentage Share of Consumption Expenditure Plus Expenditure Benefits for Different Expenditure Groups

Expenditure groups with per capita monthly consumption expenditure (Rupees)	*A sector*		*N sector*		*Overall Punjab*	
	Percentage share	*Cumulative percentage share*	*Percentage share*	*Cumulative percentage share*	*Percentage share*	*Cumulative percentage share*
1	2	3	4	5	6	7
Less than 40	1.35	1.35	0.76	0.76	1.15	1.15
40-60	11.06	12.41	8.51	9.27	10.21	11.36
60-70	9.78	22.19	8.41	17.68	9.32	20.68
70-80	10.39	32.58	9.25	26.93	10.01	30.69
80-100	17.04	49.62	18.70	45.63	17.59	48.28
100-150	30.88	80.50	29.18	74.81	30.31	78.59
150-200	11.59	92.09	12.98	87.79	12.06	90.65
200 and above	7.91	100.00	12.21	100.00	9.35	100.00
Concentration ratio	—	0.1903	—	0.2352	—	0.2030

Note: * including agricultural and non-agricultural development expenditure benefits.
A stands for agricultral sector.
N stands for non-agricultural sector.

Appendices

APPENDIX A

Projections of Population

The population figures for Punjab were estimated by using the compound growth rates worked out on the basis of 1971 and 1981 censuses. In the census of Punjab, the classification of population is done on the basis of rural and urban sectors. The breakdown of population according to agricultural and non-agricultural sectors as such is not available. Researchers have used different alternatives for the projection of population for agricultural and non-agricultural sectors.[1]

In the present study, we considered the following three alternatives in order to estimate the population for agricultural and non-agricultural sectors. Firstly on the basis of ratios of agricultural and non-agricultural workers.[2] It was based on the assumption of uniformity in the number of dependents in the two sectors. But the average size of the family is not the same in the rural and urban sectors in both censuses (1971 and 1981), so this alternative was abondoned. Secondly to work out the sex-wise ratios of workers for the agricultural and non-agricultural sectors separately and then use these ratios to arrive at the sex-wise population in the two sectors. Then adding these figures to get the sum total of population in the two sectors. Thirdly to use the ratios of agricultural and non-agricultural workers in the rural and urban sectors separately as the basis to work out the agricultural and non-agricultural population in the rural and urban sectors. Third alternative was considered to be more suitable out of three. For its application the following equations have been used:

$P = P_r + P_u$ .... (i)

Where P = total population

P_r = population in the rural sector

P_u = population in the urban sector

$P_r = R_a + R_n$ .... (ii)

Where = R_a = agricultural population in the rural sector

R_n = non-agricultural population in the rural sector.

Similarly, $P_u = U_a + U_n$

Where U_a = agricultural population in the urban sector

U_n = non-agricultural population in the urban sector.

From equations II and III we derive the following equations

$P_A = R_a + U_a$

$P_N = Ua + U_n$

where P_A and P_N stand for the agricultural and the non-agricultural population respectively. By applying this method, we got the population breakdown into agricultural and non-agricultural sectors for the years 1971 and 1981. Further the figures of agricultural and non-agricultural and population were projected with the help of compound growth rates. Table IA shows the inter-sector break-down of population during the period from 1967-68 to 1981-82.

For estimating the population in the different expenditure groups/classes of the two sectors, we used the percentages of population as revealed by the NSS Consumer Expenditure Survey (1977-78). In other words, the ratios of the rural and the urban population in the different expenditure groups were used to estimate the population in the agricultural and the non-agricultural sectors in different expenditure groups. Thus Table IIA depicts the population breakdown in different expenditure groups (1977-78).

Table IA: Estimates of Agricultural and Non-Agricultural Population in Punjab

(Lakhs)

Years	*Agricultural population*	*Non-agricultural population*	*Total population*
1967-68	79.43372	45.84013	125.27385
1968-69	80.63168	47.12647	127.75815
1969-70	81.84773	48.44399	130.29172
1970-71	83.08212	49.79342	132.87554
1971-72	84.33513	51.17547	135.51060
1972-73	85.71219	52.63451	138.34670
1973-74	87.10882	54.13333	141.24215
1974-75	88.52526	55.67295	144.19821
1975-76	89.96169	57.25445	147.21614
1976-77	91.41834	58.87888	150.29722
1977-78	92.89543	60.54736	153.44279
1978-79	94.39321	62.26099	156.65420
1979-80	95.91185	64.02096	159.93281
1980-81	97.45162	65.82842	163.28004
1981-82	99.01278	67.68477	166.69755

Table IIA: Extimated Population in Different Expenditure Groups (1977-78)

Expenditure groups with per capita monthly consumption expenditure (Rupees)	*Rural/Agricultural sector*		*Urban/Non-agricultural sector*	
	Percent-ages	*Population (Lakhs)*	*Percent-age*	*Population (Lakhs)*
Less than 40	2.78	2.582493	2.10	1.2714946
40-60	17.90	16.628282	16.50	9.9903144
60-70	13.51	12.550173	12.66	7.6652958
70-80	11.68	10.850186	11.73	7.1022053
80-100	17.73	16.47036	19.60	11.867283
100-150	25.23	23.437517	25.09	14.585859
150-200	7.49	6.9578677	8.28	5.0133214
200 and above	3.68	3.4185518	5.04	3.0515869
All groups	100	92.89543	100	60.54736

REFERENCES

1. (a) K.S.R.N.Sarma and M.J.K. Thaveraj, "Estimation of Tax Incidence in India", *Economic and Political Weekly*, (vol.VI, No.19, May 8, 1971), pp.957-964.

   (b) S.L.Shetty, "An Inter-sectoral Analysis of Taxable Capacity and Tax Burden", *Indian Journal of Agricultural Economics*, (Vol. XXVI, No. 3, July-Sept., 1971), pp. 210-246.

   (c) E.T. Mathew Agricultural Taxation and Economic Development in India. (Bombay, Asea Publishing House, 1968), p.184.

2. Here agricultural workers include those who are engaged in cultivation of land either of their own (that is, cultivators) or on wage basis (that is, agricultural labourers).

APPENDIX B

Estimates of Net State Domestic Product

To estimate the sector-wise income from 1967-68 to 1981-82, we used the revised series of Net State Domestic Product as obtained from the office of Economic Adviser. Agricultural income includes income from agriculture, livestock, forestry and fishery. It excludes income from mining and quarrying. The figures of non-agricultural income were obtained by deducting agricultural income (as defined above) from total state income. The sector-wise income and per capita income are shown in Table IB and Table IIB respectively.

Table IB: Estimates of Net State Domestic Product from the Agricultural and Non-agricultural sectors in Punjab at current prices

(Rupees crores)

Years	*Agricultural sector*	*Non-agricultural sector*	*Total*
1967-68	676.22(64.12)	378.35(35.88)	1054.57(100)
1968-69	738.39(63.33)	427.55(36.67)	1165.94(100)
1969-70	799.82(62.74)	474.97(37.26)	1274.79(100)
1970-71	833.33(60.31)	548.51(39.69)	1381.84(100)
1971-72	880.44(59.58)	597.32(40.42)	1477.76(100)

1972-73	956.44(58.49)	678.85(41.51)	1635.29(100)
1973-74	1284.00(62.77)	761.61(37.23)	2045.61(100)
1974-75	1341.10(60.60)	871.82(39.40)	2212.92(100)
1975-76	1337.97(51.48)	1260.96(48.52)	2598.93(100)
1976-77	1593.10(52.03)	1468.65(47.96)	3061.75(100)
1977-78	1742.97(50.45)	1711.77(49.55)	3454.74(100)
1978-79	1813.19(48.78)	1904.93(51.22)	3718.84(100)
1979-80	2001.22(47.43)	2218.43(52.57)	4219.65(100)
1980-81	2032.94(44.27)	2559.55(55.73)	4592.49(100)
1981-82	2502.07(43.17)	3294.57(56.83)	5796.64(100)

Note: Figures in parenthesis are percentages to total.

Table IIB: Per Capita Income in the Agricultural and Non Agricultural Sectors in Punjab (Rupees

Years	*Agricultural Sector*	*Non-agricultural Sector*	*Overall*
1967-68	851.30	825.37	841.81
1968-69	915.76	907.24	912.61
1969-70	977.20	980.45	978.41
1970-71	1003.02	1101.57	1039.95
1971-72	1043.98	1167.20	1090.51
1972-73	1115.87	1289.74	1182.02
1973-74	1474.02	1406.91	1448.30
1974-75	1514.93	1565.97	1534.64
1975-76	1487.27	2202.38	1765.38
1976-77	1742.65	2494.36	2037.13
1977-78	1876.27	2827.16	2251.13
1978-79	1921.65	3059.59	2373.92
1979-80	2086.52	3465.16	2638.39
1980-81	2086.10	3888.21	2812.65
1981-82	2527.02	4867.52	3477.34

APPENDIX C(A)

List of Items Included in the NSS consumer expenditure survey, 32nd round, July, 1977-78.

(Note: Unit of quantity is in kilograms unless specified otherwise within bracket)

Cereals and gram

1. Paddy
2. Rice
3. Chira
4. Khoi, Lawe
5. Muri
6. Rice: Sub-total (1-5)
7. Wheat
8. Ata
9. Maida
10. Suji, rawa
11. Wheat: Sub-total (7-10)
12. Jawar
13. Jowar Products
14. Jower: Sub-total (12-13)
15. Bajra
16. Bajra Products
17. Bajra: Sub-total (15-16)
18. Maize
19. Maize Products
20. Maize: Sub-total (18-19)
21. Barley
22. Barley Products
23. Barley: Sub-total (21-22)
24. Small millets
25. Small millets products

26. Small millets: Sub-total (24-25)
27. Ragi
28. Ragi Products
29. Ragi: Sub-total (27-28)
30. Total cereals: Sub-total (6+11+17+20+23+26+29)
31. Gram (Full grain)
32. Gram Products
33. Gram: Sub-total
34. Cereal substitutes

Pulses

35. Arhar (tur)
36. Gram (Split grain)
37. Moong
38. Masur
39. Urd
40. Khesari
41. Peas
42. Soyabean
43. Other pulsus
44. Pulse products
45. Pulses: Sub-total (35-41)

Milk and Milk Products

46. Milk liquid (litre)
47. Baby food (milk)
48. Milk (condensed powder)
49. Ghee
50. Butter
51. Curd
52. Ice Cream (gm)
53. Other milk products
54. Milk and milk products: sub-total (46-53)

Edible Oils

55. Vanaspati
56. Margarine
57. Mustard oil
58. Coconut oil
59. Gingelly (till) oil
60. Groundnut oil
61. Linseed oil
62. Refined oil
63. Edible oil (Others)
64. Oil seeds
65. Edible oil: Sub-total (55-64)
66. Goat meat
67. Mutton
68. Beaf
69. Pork
70. Buffalo meat
71. Other meat
72. Poultry (number)
73. Other birds (number)
74. Eggs (number)
75. Fish (fresh)
76. Fish (dry)
77. Meat, egg, fish: Sub-total (66-76)

Vegetables

78. Potato
79. Onion
80. Tomato
81. Brinjal
82. Cabbage
83. Root vegetables (arum, radish)
84. Cauliflower

85. Leafy vegetables
86. Other vegetables
87. Vegetables: Sub-total (78-86)

Fresh Fruits

88. Banana (number)
89. Lemon—orange (number)
90. Mango (number)
91. Coconut (number)
92. Guava (number)
93. Pine apple (number)
94. Grapes
95. Other fresh fruits
96. Fresh fruits: Sub-total (88-95)

Dry Fruits and Nuts

97. Cononut, Copra
98. Groundnut
99. Cashewnut
100. Dates
101. Raisin (Kish-mish, manacca etc.)
102. Other dry fruits and nuts
103. Dry fruits and nuts: Sub-total (97-102)
104. Fresh fruits and nuts: Sub-total (96-103)

Sugar

105. Sugar
106. Gur-Cane
107. Khandsari Sugar
108. Sugar candy
109. Sugar others
110. Sugar: Sub-total (105-109)

Salt

111. Sea salt
112. Rock and other salt
113. Salt: Sub-total (111-112)

Spices

114. Turmeric (gm.)
115. Black pepper (gm.)
116. Papper, dry chillies (gm.)
117. Green chillies (gm.)
118. Garlic (gm.)
119. Tamarind (gm.)
120. Ginger (gm.)
121. Curry Powder (gm.)
122. Other spices (gm.)
123. Spices: Sub-total (114-122)

Beverages and Refreshments

124. Tea (number of cups)
125. Tea leaf
126. Coffee (number of cups)
127. Coffee powder
128. Ice
129. Drinking beverages other (specify)
130. Biscuits confectioneries etc. other than cake and pastry (number)
131. Bread (number)
132. Cake and pastry (number)
133. Salted refreshments
134. Prepared sweets
135. Cooked meals (number)
136. Pickles (gm.)
137. Sauce (gm.)

138. Jam, jellies (gm.)
139. Processed food others (gm.)
140. Beverage, refreshments: Sub-total (124-139)
141. Supari (fresh) (gm.)
142. Supari (fermented) (gm.)
143. Supari (Sundried) (gm.)
144. Supari (boiled/coloured) (gm.)
145. Supari (scented) (gm.)
146. Pan leaf (number)
147. Pan finished (number)
148. Other ingredients for pan (gm.)
149. Pan: Sub-total (141-148)

Tobacco

150. Biri (number)
151. Cigarettes (number)
152. Leaf tobacco
153. Hookah tobacco
154. Cheroot (number)
155. Snuff (gm.)
156. Zardae, kimam, surti (gm.)
157. Other tobacco products (gm.)
158. Tobacco: Sub-total (150-157)

Intoxicants

159. Opium (gm.)
160. Ganja (gm.)
161. Toddy (Litre)
162. Beer (Litre)
163. Country liquor (Litre)
164. Foreign liquor (Litre)
165. Other drugs and intoxicants (gm.)
166. Intoxicants: Sub-total (159-165)
167. Pan, tobacco and intoxicants: Sub-total (149+158+166)

Fuel and Light

168. Coke
169. Coal
170. Firewood and chips
171. Electricity (st. unit)
172. Gas (st. unit)
173. Dung cake
174. Charcoal
175. Kerosene (litre)
176. Other oil used for lighting (litre)
177. Candle (number)
178. Matches (stick)
179. Methylated spirit (litre)
180. Fuel and light other
181. Fuel and light: Sub-total (168-180).

CLOTHING AND FOOTWEAR

Clothing

1. Dhoti (metre)
2. Saree (metre)
3. Cloth for shirt, pyjama, kurta, blouse, salwar etc. (metre)
4. Cloth for coat, trousers, overcoat, etc. (metre)
5. Readymade garments (number)
6. Chaddar, dopatta, wrapper, shawl (metre)
7. Headgear (metre)
8. Lungi (metre)
9. Gamcha, towel, handkerchief (number)
10. Hosiery articles, stockings, banian, underwear, bodice, etc. (number)
11. Knitted garments, sweater, pullover, cardigan, muffler, etc. (number)

12. Bedsheet, bed cover (metre)
13. Rug, blanket (metre)
14. Pillo, quilt, mattress (number)
15. Cloth for upholstery, curtain, table cloth, etc. (metre)
16. Mosquito net (number)
17. Cotton, Cotton yarn (kg.)
18. Knitting wool (gm.)
19. Mats and matting (number)
20. Clothing others (number)
21. Clothing: sub-total (1-20)

Footwear

22. Leather boots, shoe (pair)
23. Leather sandals, chappals, etc. (pair)
24. Other leather footwears (pair)
25. Other footwears (pair)
26. Footwear: sub-total (22-25) (pair)
27. Clothing and footwear: sub-total (21+26)

Miscellaneous goods and services

1. Cinema, theatre
2. Mela, fair, picnic
3. Sports goods, type etc.
4. Club fees
5. Other amusements
6. Amusements: sub-total
7. Books, journals
8. Newspapers, periodicals
9. Library charges
10. Stationery articles
11. Tuition fee (school, college)
12. Other educational expenses
13. Education: sub-total

14. Allopathic medicine
15. Homeopathic medicine
16. Ayurvedic medicine
17. Unani medicine
18. Other medicine
19. Medicine: sub-total
20. Toilet soap
21. Powder, snow, cream
22. Tooth paste, tooth powder
23. Hair oil, hair lotion, hair cream
24. Comb
25. Other toilet requisites
26. Tiolet articles
27. Shaving blades
28. Other shaving requisites
29. Electric bulbs, tube-lights
30. Electric batteries
31. Other non-durable electrical goods
32. Spectacles
33. Clock, watch
34. Torch light
35. Fountain pen
36. Lock
37. Umbrella, raincoat
38. Walking stick
39. Earthern ware
40. Plastic goods
41. Coir, rope etc.
42. Washing soap
43. Washing soda
44. Other washing requisites
45. Other petty articles
46. Sundry articles: sub-total

47. Private tuitor
48. Doctor, nurse, mid-wife
49. Domestic servant, cook
50. Sweeper
51. Barber
52. Washerman, laundry
53. Tailor
54. Priest
55. Postage, telephone
56. Other consumer services
57. Consumer services: sub-total
58. Railway fare
59. Bus, taxi fare
60. Steamer, boat fare
61. Fair for rickshaw, autorickshaw fare
62. Horocab fare
63. Hand-operated cart fare
64. Bullock cart fare
65. Portar's remuneration
66. Other hired conveyance
67. Imputed value of conveyance (owned specify)
68. Conveyance: sub-total
69. Others
70. Miscellaneous goods and services
71. House-rent, garage rent
72. Residential land rent
73. Consumer rent (other goods)
74. Consumer rent: sub-total
75. Consumer taxes and cesses

Durable Goods

1. Bedstead
2. Almirah

3. Dressing table
4. Stool, bench
5. Chair
6. Couch, sofa
7. Table, desk
8. Box, trunk
9. Suitcase, attache, kit bag
10. Foam rubber cushion (dunlop pillo type)
11. Floor matting carpet (dures)
12. Furniture (others)
13. Furniture: sub-total
14. Harmonium
15. Gramophone
16. Other musical instruments
17. Musical instruments: sub-total
18. Gold ornaments
19. Silver ornaments
20. Ornaments
21. Jewels and pearls
22. Ornaments: sub-total
23. Stainless Steel untensils
24. Bellmetal utensils
25. Copper utensils
26. Aluminium utensils
27. Iron utensils
28. Brass utensils
29. Enamel utensils
30. Crockery
31. Other utensils
32. Utensils: sub-total
33. Radio
34. Television
35. Radiogram

36. Camera and other photographic expenses
37. Tape recorder
38. Spectacles
39. Clock, watch
40. Umbrella, raincoat
41. Electric fan
42. Lamp etc.
43. Lantern lamp etc.
44. Stove
45. Pressure cooker
46. Sewing machine
47. Washing machine
48. Typewriter
49. Refrigerator
50. Air-conditioner
51. Perambulator
52. Bicycle
53. Motor cycle, scooter
54. Motor car
55. Tyres and tubes
56. Other durables (specify)
57. Other equipments: sub-total
58. Residential building and land (cost of repair only)
59. Tuition fee
60. Private tutor
61. Other educational expenses
62. Books, jounals
63. Education expenses: sub-total
64. Club fees
65. House-rent, garage rent
66. Residential land rent
67. Consumer rent: sub-total

APPENDIX C (B)

List of manufactured items (as included) in the construction of index number of wholesale prices (by groups and sub-groups)

Food products

Dairy products
Canned and preserved fruits and vegetables
Sea food
Grain mill products
Bakery products
Sugar, khandsari and gur
Sugar and confectionery, coca and chocol:te
Miscellaneous food products
Edible oils and oil cakes
Other miscellaneous food products

Beverages, tobacco and tobacco products

Wine and liquor
Soft drinks
Tobacco manufactures

Textiles

Cotton textiles
Woollen, yarn and textiles
Silk, artsilk and synthetic fibre textiles
Jute, hemp and mesta textiles
Textiles and mesta textiles
Textiles and products n.e.c.

Paper and paper products leather and, leather products

Tanned and cured finished leather
Footwear and other leather products

Rubber and rubber products

Tyre and tubes
Other rubber products

Chemical and Chemical products

Basic industrial chemicals
Fertilisers
Pesticides
Paints and varnishes
Drugs and medicines
Cosmetics, soap and detergents
Inedible oils
Synthetic resins
Dye-stuffs

Non-Metallic mineral products

Structural clay products
Glass and glass products
Earthenware and earthen pottery
Cement, lime and plaster
Miscellaneous non-metallic mineral products

Basic metals, alloys and mineral products

Basic metals and alloys
Iron, steel and ferro alloys
Non-ferrous metals and their alloys
Metal products

Machinery and transport equipment

Non-electrical machinery
Electrical machinery
Transport equipment
Motor vehicles and parts
Motor, cycles, scooters, bicycles and parts

Micellaneous products

Wood and wood products
Other manufacturing industries, n.e.c.

APPENDIX D

Methodology used for apportioning the burden for sales tax

For apportioning the burden of sales tax between agricultural and non-agricultural sectors we collected items-wise data on sales tax collection for the period from 1967-68 to 1981-82. It was made available from the office of Excise and Taxation Commissioner, Punjab. The number of items subject to sales tax under Punjab General Sales Tax (PGST) and Central Sales Tax (CST) increased from 74 (1967-68 through 1971-72) to 159 (1972-73 through 1981-82).

The consumer expenditure data compiled by National Sample Survey (NSS) (32nd round, 1977-78) Punjab, was considered to be the most suitable basis for item-wise destribution of sales tax burden. However, consumption data was available both in quantity and on value basis. We used cash-purchase expenditure on goods (and not total expenditure which included home-grown articles) on the assumption that sales tax is paid only when commoditied are purchased in cash.

The expenditure and other bases which have been used to allocate the tax burden in respect of different commodities are given below:

Sales tax item	**NSS item of consumption**
1. Automobiles and its spare parts	Conveyance expenditure on the fare including imputed value on owned conveyance
2. Air coolers	Air-conditioner
3. Arms including rifles, revolvers, pistols and ammunition	Other durables (specify)
4. Aerated water	Drinking beverages
5. Articles and wares made wholly or principally of stainless steel except razor blades and surgical instruments	Stainless steel utensils

6. Aluminium wire	Expenditure on manufactured items
7. Binoculars, telescopes and opera glasses	Other durables (specify)
8. Bicycles	Bicycles
9. Bicycles (tyres and tubes)	Bicycles
10. Bullions and its species	Ornaments
11. Bhabbar (Bhuggar, kahi)	Expenditure on manufactured items
12. Beer	
13. Bardana	Cash expenditure
14. Bricks	Expenditure on consumer rent
15. Bread and all other bakery goods, prepared with the help of powder	Bread, biscuits, cake and pastry
16. Bamboo and its products	Expenditure on manufactured items
17. Bitumen (Oradator)	Expenditure on food, cash and expenditure on bus, taxi fars.
18. Blankets and rugs	Rug, blankets
19. Baby milk and baby food sold in sealed container	Baby food and milk (condenced powder)
20. Brassware	Brass utensils
21. Betal nuts	Supari (betal nuts)
22. Cotton whether ginned or pressed, unginned baled or otherwise	Cotton, cotton yarn
23. Cotton thread	Cotton, cotton yarn
24. Cotton and cotton yarn waste	Cotton, cotton yarn
25. Cotton and cotton yarn waste and pillow covers	Cotton, cotton yarn
26. Cotton yarn	Cotton, cotton yarn
27. Carpets	Floor matting, carpet and duree
28. Chillies	Pepper, dry chillies

29. Coal including cake infill its items	Coal
30. Charcoal	Charcoal
31. Confectioner goods	Buscuits, confectionery etc. other than cake and pastry.
32. Cigarette cases and lighters	Cigarettes
33. Cinematographic equipment including camera, projectors and sound recording and reproducing equipments, lenses, films and parts and accessories required for use therewith	Expenditure on cinema
34. Clock, time pieces and watches, including straps and chains of watches	Clock, watch
35. Cutlery including knives, forks and spoons	Other untensils
36. Chemicals	Other washing requisites and other petty articles
37. Cosmetics, perfumery and toilet goods including hair oils, hair tonic and hair cream	Toilet articles
38. Cement excluding cement articles	Consumer rent
39. Cement articles other than cement	Consumer rent
40. Cotton hosiery products	Hosiery articles, stockings, banian, underwear, bodies etc.
41. Caustic soda and soda ash	Expenditure on washing soda, washing soaps and other washing requisities
42. Guilinery and flavouring	Non-food cash expenditure

43. Copper and bronze utensils	Bell metal and copper utensils
44. Condensed milk	Milk (condenced powder)
45. Cheese and butter	Butter
46. Durees	Floor matting, carpet and duree
47. Dry fruits	Dry fruits and nuts
48. Dictaphone and other similar apparatus for recording sound, spare parts thereof	Expenditure on cinema
49. Drugs and medicines	Medicines
50. Edible oils other than vanaspati	Edible oil (others)
51. Electric valves accumulaters amplifiers and loud speakers and spare parts and accessories	Other non-durable electric goods
52. Electric goods	Electric bulbs, tube lights, electric batteries, other non-durable electric goods
53. Electric fans	Electric fan
54. Electric goods other than electric equipments and other accessories including service metres required for generator and transmission	Electric bulbs, tube lights, electric batteries, other non-durable electric goods
55. Eatables and non-alcoholic portable liquor, such as fruit syrups, juices, jams etc. fruits and juices distilled (arks) essence corn flaks wheat flake (etc. packed in tins or bottles or plastic containers or sealed packing of any kind)	Pickles, sauce, jams and jelly, processed food others.

56. Fur and articles of personal and domestic use made from furs	Readymade garments
57. Foodgrains of all kinds (other than wheat and its flour, maize and its flour rice and paddy)	Consumption of foodgrains of all kinds and (other than wheat and its flour, maize and its flour, rice and paddy).
58. A. Wheat and its flour	Wheat and Atta
B. Maize and its flour	Maize and its products
C. Rice	Rice
D. Paddy	Rice
59. Foreign liquor	Foreign liquor
60. Fire wood	Fire wood
61. Furniture of iron and steel including safe almirahs	Almirah, couch and sofa
62. Furniture (other than that or iron and steel)	Dressing table, chair, couch and sofa
63. Fire extinguisher	Expenditure on manufactured items
64. Footwears (other than leather shoes)	Other footwear
65. Fountain pens all pencils	Fountain pen
66. Fire works	Non-food cash expenditure
67. Foam rubber products	Expenditure on foam rubber, cushion
68. Furnace oil	Expenditure on manufactured items
69. Garments readymade	Readymade garments
70. Garments of pure silk cloth	Readymade garments
71. Garments knitted	Knitted garments and knitting wool
72. Groundnuts	Groundnuts
73. Ghee other than vegetable ghee	Ghee

74. Gur	Gur
75. Gramophone and component parts thereof and records	Other durables
76. Glassware and chinaware including crockery	Crockery
77. Gas cylinder and cooking gas	Gas (Fuel and light: sub-total)
78. Gotas, gota kinarah, salma sitaras, etc.	Readymade garments
79. Gold and silver wares	Gold ornaments and silver ornaments
80. Glass bangles	Toilet articles
81. Hardware	Non-food cash expenditure
82. Hides and skins (whether raw and dressed)	Expenditure and leather boots, shoes, sandals, chappals and other leather footwear
83. Iron and steel	Expenditure on manufactured items
84. Ivory ore	Expenditure on manufactured items
85. Ivory goods	Ornaments: sub-total
86. Iron sheets	Expenditure on manufactured items
87. Jewellery containing precious, semi-precious stones	Ornaments: sub-total
88. Knitting wool	Knitting wool
89. Karyana goods	Non-food cash expenditure
90. Kerosene oil and light diesel oil	Kerosene
91. Lubricants including mobile oils	Non-food cash expenditure
92. Leather shoes	Leather boots, shoes

93. Margarine	Margarine
94. Maida and suji	Maida and suji
95. Leather goods (other than shoes)	Leather sandles, chappals and other leather footwear
96. Matches	Matches
97. Molasses	Country liquor
98. Metallic utensils (other than steel)	Utensils: sub-total
99. Metals	Utensils: sub-total
100. Motor vehicles including chassis or motor vehicles, other accesories motor tyre and tubes and their parts thereof	Bus, taxi fare
101. Motor cycle and motor cycles combinations and motor scooters and tyres (tubes accessories and spare parts combinations, motor scooters and motorrettes).	Motor cycles, scooter, motor care
102. Motor vehicles tyres and tubes	Motor vehicles, tyres and tubes
103. Machines run by electric power	Electric bulbs, tube lights, electric batteries, other non-durable electric goods
104. Mica	Expenditure on manufactured items
105. Marble and articles made of Marble including marble chips	Consumer rent
106. Musical instruments	Musical instruments: sub-total
107. Ornaments except silver ornaments and jewellery (other than jewellery) containing precious stones	Ornaments: sub-total

108. Oilseeds other than ground nuts	Oil seeds
109. Oil cakes	Milk (liquid)
110. Pulses of all kinds	Cash expenditure on pulses
111. Pile carpets	Floor matting (carpet, durees)
112. Petroleum products	Expenditure on manufactured items
113. Photographic and other cameras, enlarger lenses films and plates and cloth and other part and accessories	Expenditure on camera and other photographic expenses
114. Parambulators	Parambulators
115. Picnic sets	Crockery
116. Plastic celluloid bakelite goods and goods of a similar substance except toys of children and plastic footwear	Plastic goods
117. Pesticides	Expenditure (gross) on agricultural commodities.
118. Potash and other explosive	Other petty articles
119. Plywood and hard board card and straw board	Furniture
120. Playing cards	Other amusements
121. Raw wool	Knitting wool
122. Readymade umbrella cloth	Other Sundry articles
123. Readymade hosiery goods (except cotton waste)	Hosiery articles, stockings, banyans
124. Refrigerators and air-conditioning plants and components parts thereof	Other durables (specify)
125. Rubber goods	Furniture
126. Rerolling goods products	Expenditure on manufactured items

127. Resin	Expenditure on manufactured items
128. Razor and razor blades	Shaving blades
129. Rain coats, umbrella hat covers	Other petty articles
130. Shakar	Khandsari sugar
131. Sound transmitting equipments including telephones and loudspeakers and spare parts	Non-food cash expenditure
132. Sewing machines	Sewing machines
133. Scientific instruments	Non-food cash expenditure
134. Sanitary goods and fittings and water supplying materials	Consumer rent
135. Silver ornaments and jewellery	Silver ornaments, jewels and pearls
136. Sports goods	Sports goods, toys etc.
137. Soap of all varieties including tooth paste toilet soap and washing soap	Toilet soap, tooth-paste, tooth powder and washing soap
138. Springs of all kinds intended force by the medical profession	Expenditure on total medical items
139. Spectacles and lenses, gogals and glasses rough blank and spectacles frames and parts and spare parts and accessories used	Spectacles
140. Stoves of all kinds, pressure lamps, spare parts and accessories	Stove, pressure cooker
141. Steel trunks and steel bags and case made of steel or aluminium	Box and trunks

142. Stationery goods	Stationery articles
143. Tea and coffee	Tea leaf and coffee powder
144. Tiles including neoasic tiles (but excluding roofing tiles leminations seats and sunmica sheets)	Consumer rent
145. Tractors judiegenions imported	Expenditure (Gross) on agricultural commodities
146. Typewriters / training machines	Non-food cash expenditure
147. Tape records and spare parts thereof	Tape recorders
148. Tansmitters	Other equipment
149. Timber	Consumer rent
150. Tape, newar and laces	Expenditure on furniture
151. Umbrella cloth of pure silk	Other petty articles
152. Vegetable Ghee	Ghee
153. Vacuum flask	Other durables (specify)
154. Varnishing and paints	Expenditure on total rent plus total furniture
155. Woolen yarn (other than knitting wool)	Knitting wool
156. Water coolers	Other durables (specify)
157. Wireless reception instruments and apparatus including televisions	Gramophones, radiograms and television
158. White printing paper	Sanitary articles
159. Water pumps and water pumping sets compressors	NSS cash expenditure
160. Zari thread and embriodery materials of gold silver	Readymade garments
161. Miscellaneous	NSS cash expenditure

APPENDIX E

Minimum consumption expenditure in the Rural punjab based on the consumer price index numbers for agricultural labourers

Years	*Consumer price index numbers*	*Minimum consumption expenditure (Rs. per capita)*
1967-68	100	468.59
1968-69	98.45	461.33
1969-70	101.03	473.42
1970-71	100.00	468.59
1971-72	105.15	492.72
1972-73	112.37	526.55
1973-74	140.72	659.40
1974-75	173.71	803.99
1975-76	158.76	743.93
1976-77	157.22	736.72
1977-78	171.13	811.90
1978-79	171.65	804.33
1979-80	192.78	903.35
1980-81	225.26	1055.55
1981-82	239.17	1120.73

APPENDIX F

Minimum Consumption Expenditure in the urban Punjab based on index number (unweighted) of wholesale prices of 50 (Agricultural and industrial) commodities

Years	*General index*	*Minimum consumption expenditure (Rs. per capita)*
1967-68	100	518.09
1968-69	97.44	504.83
1969-70	102.71	532.13
1970-71	100.72	521.82
1971-72	101.38	525.24
1972-73	113.67	588.91
1973-74	141.52	733.20
1974-75	181.62	940.95
1975-76	169.94	880.44
1976-77	161.34	835.88
1977-78	189.04	979.40
1978-79	184.64	956.60
1979-80	213.41	1105.65
1980-81	259.91	1346.56
1981-82	281.46	1458.21

APPENDIX G

Revenue from passenger tax and goods tax in Punjab

(Lakh Rupees)

Years	*Passenger tax*	*Goods tax*	*Total*
1967-68	305.89	76.47	382.36
	(80.00)	(20.00)	(100.00)
1968-69	361.25	90.31	451.56
	(80.00)	(20.00)	(100.00)
1969-70	482.39	120.60	602.99
	(80.00)	(20.00)	(100.00)
1970-71	587.73	146.93	734.66
	(80.00)	(20.00)	(100.00)
1971-72	661.10	165.28	826.38
	(80.00)	(20.00)	(100.00)
1972-73	767.62	144.47	912.08
	(84.16)	(15.84)	(100.00)
1973-74	906.40	214.00	1120.40
	(80.90)	(19.10)	(100.00)
1974-75	1102.58	259.13	1361.71
	(80.97)	(19.03)	(100.00)
1975-76	1270.38	247.58	1517.96
	(83.69)	(16.31)	(100.00)
1976-77	1473.59	209.36	1682.95
	(87.56)	(12.44)	(100.00)
1977-78	1731.51	197.10	1928.61
	(89.78)	(10.22)	(100.00)
1978-79	1920.59	194.60	2115.19
	(90.80)	(9.20)	(100.00)
1979-80	2073.93	237.86	2311.79
	(89.71)	(10.29)	(100.00)
1980-81	2356.00	261.87	2617.87
	(90.00)	(10.00)	(100.00)
1981-82	2959.15	296.05	3255.21
	(90.90)	(9.10)	(100.00)

Note: Figures in parenthesis are percentage shares.
Source: Excise and Taxation Commissioner, Punjab.

APPENDIX H

Per Capita Cash Expenditure And Expenditure On Manufactured Items For Different Expenditure Groups In Agricultural And Non-Agricultural Sectors In Punjab

(Rs. per month)

Expenditure groups with per capita monthly consumption expenditure (Rupees)	*Rural Sector*			*Urban Sector*		
	Expenditure on manufactured items	*Cash expenditure*	*Total expenditure*	*Expenditure on manufactured items*	*Cash expenditure*	*Total expenditure*
Less than 40	9.57	27.51	39.07	6.94	19.43	36.54
40-60	12.79	43.63	51.26	16.26	53.56	55.60
60-70	17.18	50.30	63.87	18.35	68.38	69.14
70-80	18.51	43.39	75.01	21.44	72.80	73.60
80-100	27.52	57.44	84.41	27.25	74.38	86.18
100-150	30.08	52.04	118.45	48.14	122.76	124.81
150-200	53.03	122.84	164.07	53.52	153.51	162.16
200 and above	103.99	158.37	237.79	124.01	254.068	194.92
All groups	30.20	60.11	93.54	32.58	88.26	102.58

Source: NSS Consumer Expenditure Survey 32nd Round, 1977-78

APPENDIX I

Percentages of Expenditure On Education At Various Stages In Punjab

Years	*Primary Education*	*Secondry Education*	*Others**	*Total*
1967-68	35.32	46.57	18.11	100.00
1968-69	33.45	47.36	19.19	100.00
1969-70	28.34	49.99	21.67	100.00
1970-71	26.70	49.70	23.60	100.00
1971-72	26.11	50.95	22.94	100.00
1972-73	26.68	56.28	17.04	100.00
1973-74	28.73	56.32	14.95	100.00
1974-75	31.83	53.63	14.54	100.00
1975-76	38.54	46.68	14.78	100.00
1976-77	39.36	45.92	14.72	100.00
1977-78	41.56	43.02	15.42	100.00
1978-79	40.25	42.34	17.41	100.00
1979-80	37.27	46.30	16.43	100.00
1980-81	39.20	48.59	12.21	100.00
1981-82	36.97	46.81	16.22	100.00

* Others include expenditure on special education, university and other education, sport and youth welfare general and technical education.

Source: Punjab Government Budgets.

APPENDIX J

Index Number Of Whole Sale Prices (Weighted) Of 21 Agricultural Commodities Grown In Punjab

(Base: 1967-68=100)

Years	*General Index*
1967-68	100.00
1968-69	106.78
1969-70	105.86
1970-71	103.82
1971-72	105.81
1972-73	113.20
1973-74	136.34
1974-75	174.16
1975-76	162.44
1976-77	153.47
1977-78	177.12
1978-79	167.23
1979-80	180.33
1980-81	231.09
1981-82	256.98

Bibliography

R.K. Amin, "Agricultural Taxation and Resource Mobilisation", *Artha Vikas*, (Vol. 5, July, 1969), pp.154-170.

A.C.Angrish, "Agricultural and Non-agricultural Taxation: An Estimate of their Burden in Rajasthan", *Economic and Political Weekly*, (vol. 5, January 10, 1970), pp. 59-66.

__________, "Direct Agricultural Tax Burden, Inter-State Comparison", *Economic and Political Weekly*, (Vol. IV, No. 34, August 23, 1969).

__________, "*Direct Taxation of Agriculture in India: With Special Reference to Land Revenue and Agricultural Income Tax*, (Bombay, Somaiya Publications, Pvt. Ltd., 1972).

__________, Rationalised Agricultural Tax Structure in India and Some Policy Implications", *Artha Vikas*, (Vol. 5, July, 1969), pp.154-170.

Sen Bandhudas, "The Role of Agriculture's Contributions in the Theory of Economic Growth in Over-Populated Countries", *Indian Journal of Agricultural Economics*, (vol. 22, No.4, October-December, 1967).

R.K.Bansal and J.R.Gupta, *Economic Aspects of Sales Tax: A Case Study of Punjab*, (New Delhi, Atlantic Publishers and Distributors, 1965).

Paul Baran, *The Political Economy of Growth*, (New York, Monthly Review Press, 1957).

P.K.Bardhan, "Agriculture Inadequately Taxed", *Economic Weekly*, (Vol. 13, December 9, 1961), pp.1829-1835.

__________, "On the Incidence of Poverty in Rural India", *Economic and Political Weekly*, (Annual Number, 1973).

G.S.Bhalla, *Changing Agrarian Structure in India,* (New Delhi, Meenakshi Prakashan, 1974).

P.K.Bhargava, "Incidence of Agricultural Taxation: Scope for Raising Additional Resources", *Commerce,* (October 1, 1966).

__________, *Taxation of Agriculture in India,* (Bombay, Vora and Company, 1976).

R.N.Bhargava, *Indian Public Finance,* (London, Allen and Unwin, 1962).

Jatinder Bhatia, "Agricultural Land Taxation in Punjab", *Economic and Political Weekly*, (Vol. IV, January 18, 1969), pp. 211-215.

B.B.Bhattacharya, "Taxing the Rural Rich: It's an Immediate Task", *Yojana*, (Vol. 30, No.16, September 1-15, 1986), pp.8-10.

Richard M.Bird, "Agricultural Taxation in Developing Countries", *Finance and Development*, (September, 1974), pp.35-37.

__________, *Taxing Agricultural Land in Developing Countries.* (Baltimore, The Johns Hopkins Press, 1964).

__________, and Luc Henry De Wulf, "Taxation and Income Distribution in Latin America - A Critical Review of Empirical Studies", *International Monetary Fund Staff Papers*, (vol. 20, November, 1973), pp.639-682.

P.R.Brahmananda, *Productivity in the Indian Economy: Rising Inputs for Falling Outputs,* (Delhi, Himalya Publishing House, November, 1982).

T.J.Byres, "Land Reform, Industrialization and the Marketed surplus in India: An Essay on the Power of Rural Bias", in David Lehmann (ed.) *Agrarian Reform and Reformism*

Studies of Peru, Chile, China and India, (London, Faber and Faber Ltd., 1974), pp. 224-225.

G.K.Chadha, *The State and Rural Economic Transformation: The Case of Punjab, 1950-85*, (New Delhi, Sage Publications India, Pvt. Ltd., 1986).

P.K.Chatterjee, and Shibdas Banerjee, "Surplus Labour in West Bengal's Agriculture - A Note", *Indian Journal of Agricultural Economics*, (Vol.30, No.3, July-September, 1975) pp. 60-61.

Raja J. Chelliah, *Fiscal Policy in Underdeveloped Countries With Special Reference to India*, (London, George Allen and Unwin, 1962).

__________,"Trends in Taxation in Developing Countries", *International Monetary Fund Staff Papers*, (Vol.18, July, 1971), pp.254-331.

__________, and Ram N.Lal, *Incidence of Indirect Taxation in India, 1973-74*, (New Delhi, National Institute of Public Finance and Policy, 1978).

James Cutt, *Taxation and Economic Development in India*, (Delhi, Vikas Publications, 1969).

Huge Dalton, *Principles of Public Finance*, (London, Routledge and Kegan Paul, 1936).

V.M.Dandekar, "Prices, Production and Marketed Surplus of Foodgrains", *Indian Journal of Agricultural Economics*, (vol. 19, Nos. 3 and 4, July-December, 1964), pp.186-195.

__________, and Nilkantha Rath, "Poverty in India", *Economic and Political Weekly*, (vol.6, No.1, January 2, 1971), pp.25-48.

M.L.Dantwala, "Agricultural Policy since Independence", *Indian Journal of Agricultural Economics*, (vol. 31, No.4, October-December, 1976), pp.31-53.

Bhabatosh Datta, "Indirect Taxes in a Developing Economy",

Capital, (Mid Year Special, August 31, 1981), pp.15-17.

K.L.Datta, *Measurement of Poverty in India-Statewise Estimates*, (New Delhi, Perspective Planning Division, Planning Commission, Paper 11/22, Presented on First National Conference on Social Sciences, January 12-15, 1981).

V.G.Desai, "Two Measures of Surplus Mobilisation in Indian Agriculture", *Asian Economic Review*, (vol. 8, No.4, August, 1966), pp.461-478.

Luc De Wulf, "Fiscal Incidence Studies in Developing Countries Survey and Critique," *International Monetary Fund Staff Papers,* (vol. 22, March, 1975).

Ashok Dhar, *Domestic Terms of Trade and Economic Development of India 1952-53 to 1964-65,* (Ithaca, Cornell University, 1967).

K.S.Dhindsa, and Jaspal Singh, "Marketed Surplus of Wheat and Paddy by Farm Size in Punjab - A Case Study", *Margin*, (vol. 15, No.2, January, 1983), pp.81-88.

M.Dobb, *On Economic Theory and Socialism: Collected Papers*, (London and Boston, Routlege and Keganpaul Ltd., 1955).

G.S.Dorrance, "The Income Terms of Trade", *Review of Economic Studies, (1948-49)*, pp. 50-56.

D.N.Dwivedi, "Incidence of Land Revenue in Uttar Pradesh", *Economic and Political Weekly*, (vol. 3, June 8, 1968), pp. 871-72.

__________, *Problems and Prospects of Agricultural Taxation in Uttar Pradesh*, (New Delhi, People's Publishing House, 1973).

__________, *Readings in Indian Public Finance*, (Delhi, Chanakya Publications, 1981).

__________, "Taxable Capacity of Agricultural Sector", *Economic and Political Weekly*, (vol. 3, No.50, December 14, 1968).

Carl Eicher and Lawrence Witt (ed.), *Agriculture in Economic Development,* (New York, McGraw Hill, Book Company, 1964).

Francine R.Frankel, *India's Green Revolution: Economic Gains and Political Costs,* (Bombay, Oxford University Press, 1971).

Ved P. Gandhi, "Agricultural Taxation Policy: Search for Direction", *Artha Vikas*, (vol. 5, July, 1969), pp.3-49.

__________, *Some Aspects of India's Tax Structure*, (Bombay, Vora and Company, 1970).

__________, *Tax Burden on Indian Agriculture,* (Ph.D.Thesis presented to the Harvard University, Cambridge, Massachusetts, May, 1964).

__________, "Taxation of Farm Income: A Comment", *The Economic Times,* (Annual, 1974), pp. 130-141.

M.V.George and A.J. Singh, "Role of Agriculture and Strategy for Agricultural Development in Over-Populated Countries", *Indian Journal of Agricultural Economics,* (vol. 22, No.4, October-December, 1967).

R.N.Ghosh, *Agriculture in Economic Development with Special Reference to Punjab,* (New Delhi, Vikas Publishing House Pvt. Ltd., 1977).

Richard Grabowski and Yoon Bong Joon, "Inter-sectoral Resource Flows and Economic Development: The Case of India", *Indian Journal of Agricultural Economics,* (October-December, 1982) pp. 502-510.

S.S.Grewal and P.S.Rangi, "Wheat Cultivation: Economics of Punjab State", *The Economic Times*, (August 26, 1982), p.5.

H.M.Grover and M.C.Madhvan, "Agricultural Taxation and India's Third Five-Year Plan", *Land Economics,* (vol.38, No.1, 1962), pp.57-59.

I.S.Gulati, *Resource Prospects of the Third Five-Year Plan*, (Bombay, Orient Longman's Ltd., 1960).

Anand P. Gupta, "Income Distribution, Tax Yield, and Progression in Income Taxation", *Economic and Political Weekly*, (vol. 7, October 14, 1972), pp. 2111-2118.

J.R.Gupta, *Burden of Tax in Punjab - An Inter-Sector and Inter-Class Analysis*, (New Delhi, Concept Publishing Company, 1982).

Ursula K. Hicks, *Public Finance,* (Cambridge, Cambridge University Press, 1946).

Y.Haung, "Distribution of Tax Burden in Tanzania", *The Economic Journal*, (vol. 86, March, 1976), pp.73-86.

P.C.Jain, *Agricultural Taxation in Haryana*, (Kurukshetra, Kurukshetra University Press, 1974).

Rajendra Jain, *State Taxation in India,* (Bhopal, Progress Publishers, 1972).

S.S. Johl, "Agricultural Taxation in a Developing Economy: A Case of India", *Indian Journal of Agricultural Economics*, (vol. 27, No.3, July-September, 1972).

___________, "Gains of the Green Revolution: How they have been shared in Punjab". *Journal of Development Studies,* (vol. 2, No. 3, April, 1975), pp.178-189.

B.F.Johnston, and J.W.Mellor, "The Role of Agriculture in Economic Development", *American Economic Review*, (vol. 51, No.4, September, 1961).

D.W.Jorgenson, "The Development of a Dual Economy", *Economic Journal,* (Vol. 71, June, 1961), pp.309-334.

M.D.Joshi, (ed.), *Mobilisation of State Resources*, (New Delhi, Implex India, 1967).

T.M.Joshi, N.Anjanaiah and S.V.Behnde, *Studies in the Taxation of Agricultural Land and Income in India*, (London, Asia Publishing House, 1968).

A.S.Kahlon, *Agricultural Price Policy in India,* (New Delhi, Allied Publishers Pvt.Ltd., 1983).

__________, *Modernization of Punjab Agriculture,* (New Delhi, Allied Publishers Pvt. Ltd., 1984).

__________, and D.S.Tyagi, "Inter-Sectoral Terms of Trade", *Economic and Political Weekly*, (vol. 15, No. 52, December 27, 1980), pp.A-173 to A-184.

G.S.Kainth, "Changing Pattern of Sectoral Distribution of Income in Indian Economy: 1960-61 and 1977-78", *Margin*, (vol. 12, No.4, July, 1980), pp. 63-73.

Harjeet kaur, *Taxation and Development Finance in India,* (New Delhi, Classical Publishing Co., 1992).

Rajbans Kaur, *Agricultural Pricing Policies in Developing Countries,* (New Delhi, Kalyani Publishers, 1984).

N.A.Khan, "Resource Mobilisation from Agriculture and Economic Development in India", *Economic Development and Cultural Change,* (Vol. 12, October, 1963), pp.42-54.

Raj Krishna, "Inter-sectoral Equity and Agricultural Taxation in India", *Economic and Political Weekly,* (Special Number, August, 1972).

S.N.Krishnan, "The Marketable Surplus of Foodgrains", *Economic and Political Weekly*, (vol.17, Annual Number, February, 1965).

Ram Kumar, M.L.Sharma and G.S.Sisodia, "Mobilisation of Rural Surplus - A Study of Savings in Rural Hissar", *Indian Journal of Agricultural Economics*, (Vol.30 No. 3, July-September, 1975), pp.16-25.

D.T. Lakdawala and K.V. Nambiar, *Commodity Taxation in India,* (Ahmedabad, Sardar Patel Institute of Economics and Social Research, 1972).

__________, and K.V. Nambiar, "Resource Mobilization in Gujarat", *Commerce,* (vol. 122, No. 3115, January 16, 1971) p. 116.

Harvey Leibenstein, *Economic Backwardness and Economic Growth,* (New York, John Willey, 1957).

John Macrae, "The relationship between Agricultural and Industrial Growth with Special Reference to the Development of the Punjab Economy from 1950 to 1965", *Journal of Development Studies,* (vol. 7, No. 4, July 1971), pp. 397-421.

E.T. Mathew, *Agricultural Taxation and Economic Development in India,* (London, Asia Publishing House, 1968).

P.N. Mathur, and H. Ezekeil, "Marketable Surplus of Food and Price Fluctuations in a Developing Economy", *Kyklos,* (vol. 14, 1961), pp. 396-408.

B.S. Minhas, "Rural Poverty, Land Redistribution and Development", *Indian Economic Review,* (vol. 5, No. 1, April, 1970).

A.C. Minocha, "Surplus Flows in Indian Economy II: Political Courage Needed to Tap Agricultural Savings", *Commerce,* (June 17, 1967), pp. 1066-1067.

Ashok Mitra, "Estimation of Surplus Labour in Agriculture and Problems in Mobilization", *Indian Journal of Agricultual Economics,* (vol. 30, No. 3, July-September, 1975).

----------------, *Terms of Trade and Class Relations,* (New Jersey, Frank Case and Co., 1977).

Ashok Mody, "Resource Flows between Agriculture and Non-Agriculture: Critique of an Estimate", *Indian Journal of Agricultural Economics,* (vol. 34, No. 4, October-December, 1979).

V.G. Mutalik, "Two Measures of Surplus Mobilisation in Indian Agriculture", *Asian Economic Review,* (August, 1966), pp. 461-478).

M.V. Nadkarni, *Marketable Surplus and Market Dependence in a Millet Region,* (Allied Publishers Pvt. Ltd. 1980).

Shyam, Nath, "Incidence of Taxation in Rajasthan", *Margin,* (vol. 12, April, 1980), pp. 60-73.

N.C.A.E.R., *Incidence of Taxation in Gujarat,* (New Delhi, 1970).

------------------, *Incidence of Taxation in Mysore State,* (New Delhi, 1972).

W.H. Nicholls, "An Agricultural Surplus as a Factor in Economic Development", *Journal of Political Economy,* (vol. 71, No. 1, Fabruary, 1963), pp. 1-29.

-------------------, "The Place of Agriculture in Economic Development", in Eicher and Witt (ed.) *Agiculture in Economic Development,* (New York, McGraw Hill, 1964), pp. 11-44.

R. Nurkse, *Problems of Capital Formation in Underdeveloped Countries,* (New York, Oxford University Press, 1953).

T. Mahesh, *Pathak and Arun S. Patel, Agricultural Taxation in Gujarat,* (Bombay, Asia Publishing House, 1968).

Ramayan Prasad, *Agricultural Taxation and Economic Development,* (New Delhi, Deep and Deep Publications, 1987).

K. Raj, "Inter-sectoral Equity and Agricultural Taxation in India", *Economic and Political Weekly,* (vol. 6, Special Number, 1972).

K.N. Raj, "Direct Taxation of Indian Agriculture", *Indian Economic Review,* (vol. 7, No. 5, April, 1973).

------------------, "Resources for the Third Plan - An Approach", *Economic Weekly,* (Annual Number, vol. 11, January, 1959), pp. 203-208.

A.N. Rajamani, "Agricultural, Non-Agricultural Relative Tax Burden", *Asian Economic Review,* (vol. 6, No. 1, November, 1963), pp. 56-72.

C.H. Hanumantha Rao, *Taxation of Agricultural Land in Andhra Pradesh,* (Bombay, Asia Publishing House, 1962).

T. Divakara Rao, *Tax Burden in Indian Economy,* (New Delhi, Criterian Publications, 1984).

Hemlata Rao, "Tax Incidence on Agricultural Sector in Uttar Pradesh", *Economic and Politcal Weekly,* (vol. 6, September 11, 1971), pp. 1961-1968.

K.N. Reddy, *Tax Burden on Agriculture in India (An Enquiry into the Feasibility of Agricultural Income-Tax),* (Baroda, Good Companians Publishers, 1972).

K.N. Reddy, *The Growth of Public Expenditure in India,* (Delhi Sterling Publishers, Pvt. Ltd., 1972).

G.S. Sahota, *Indian Tax Structure and Economic Development,* (New Delhi, Asia Publishing House, 1961).

K.S.R.N. Sarma and M.J.K. Thavaraj, "Estimation of Tax Incidence in India", *Economic and Political Weekly,* (vol. 6, May 8, 1971), pp. 957-964.

Prem S. Sharma, "Estimation of Marketable Surplus of Foodgrains by Size-Classes of Holdings in Rural Cultivating Households - A Physical Approach", *Agricultural Situation in India,* (vol. 27, No. 5, August, 1972), pp. 327-335.

S.L. Shetty, "An Inter-Sectoral Analysis of Taxable Capacity and Tax Burden", *Indian Journal of Agricultural Economics,* (vol. 26, July-September, 1971), pp. 216-246.

------------------, "Inter-Class Incidence of Taxation in Farm and Non-Farm Sectors in India", *Economic and Political Weekly,* (vol. 6, No. 52, December 25, 1971), pp. A -173 to A-186.

------------------, "Recent Trends in Inter-Sectoral Terms of Trade" *Economic and Political Weekly,* (June 19, 1971) pp. 1235-1240.

Ayodhya Singh, "Mobilization of State Resources from Agricultural Sector", in M.D. Joshi (ed.), *Mobilization of State Resources,* (New Delhi, Impex India, 1967).

M.L. Singh, *Sectoral Terms of Trade and Economic Growth in India,* (New Delhi, Sterling Publishers Pvt. Ltd., 1976).

Adam Smith, *An Inquiry into the Nature and Causes of the Wealth of Nations,* edited by Edwin Cannan (New York, The Modern Library, 1937).

F.W. Taussig, *International Trade,* (New York, Macmillan, 1927).

R. Thamarajakshi, "Inter-Sectoral Terms of Trade and Marketed Surplus of Agricultural Produce 1951-52 to 1965-66", *Economic and Political Weekly,* (vol. 4, No. 26, June 28, 1969), pp. A - 91 to A - 102.

G. Thimmiah, "Taxable Capacity of Agricultural Sector", *Economic and Political Weekly,* (Feburary, 1969).

D.S. Tyagi, "Farm Prices and Class Bias in India", *Economic and Political Weekly,* (vol. 24, No. 39, September 29, 1979), pp. A - 111 to A - 124.

J.S. Uppal, *India's* Economic Problems: An Analytical Approach, (New Delhi, Tata McGraw-Hill, Publishing Company, 1975).

C.N. Vakil and P.R. Brahmananda, *Planning for an Expanding Economy,* (Bombay, Vora and Company Publishers Pvt. Ltd., 1956).

Jacob Viner, *Studies in the Theory of International Trade,* (New York, Harper and Row, 1937).

H.R. Wagstaff, "The Economic Surplus of Agriculture in the United Kingdom", *Journal of Agricultural Economics,* (vol. 23, No. 3, September, 1972).

Luc De Wulf, "Fiscal Incidence Satudies in Developing Countries: Survey and Technique", *IMF Staff Papers,* (vol. 22, No. 1, March, 1975), pp. 61-131.

Mohammad Zahir, *Public Expenditure and Income Distribution in India,* (New Delhi, Associated Publishing House, 1972).

REPORTS AND OTHER OFFICIAL PUBLICATIONS

Government of India, Ministry of Finance, *Report of the Taxation Inquiry Commission*, 1953-54, (New Delhi, Vol. I, 1955).

Government of India, Ministry of Finance, *Incidence of Indirect Taxation, 1958-59*, (New Delhi, 1960).

Government of India, Ministry of Finance, *Incidence of Indirect Taxation, 1963-64,* (New Delhi, 1969).

Government of India, Ministry of Finance, *Report of the Indirect Taxation Inquiry Committee,* (New Delhi, October, 1977 and January, 1978), vol. I-II.

Government of India, Planning Commission, *Five-Year Plans,* (First to Eighth).

Government of India, Ministry of Finance, *Economic Survey* (Annual).

Government of Punjab, *Economics of Agricultural Production and Farm Management in Punjab, 1967-68 to 1969-70* (Combined Report), Mimeographed.

Government of Punjab, *Various Statistical Abstracts.*

Government of Punjab, *Various Statistical Abstracts of Public Finance.*

Government of Punjab, *Punjab Government Budgets.*

Government of Punjab, *Index Number of Parity, Publication* No. 402.

Government of Punjab, *Report of the Taxation Enquiry and Resource Committee,* Punjab (1971).

Reserve Book of India, Reports on Currency and Finance.